Landscaping for Water Conservation: XERISCAPE!

City of Aurora, Colorado
Utilities Department

Editor: Kimberley M. Knox,
            Water Conservation Technician
            Aurora Utilities Department

Jointly published by:
City of Aurora, CO

Denver Water Department, Denver, CO

Cover Photo
Summer Xeriscape on the Front Range
James Knopf, Landscape Architect, Boulder

Back Photo
Winter Scene of Same Home
James Knopf, Landscape Architect, Boulder

ISBN 0-9622900-1-7
Library of Congress
Catalog Card Number 89-060959

This book printed on recycled paper

March 8, 1989

"In our semi-arid climate, wise water use must become a way of life. We can no longer afford to view water management only in terms of developing new supplies of water. We need to promote a conservation ethic in Colorado and make water conservation a statewide priority."

Roy Romer, Governor

Preface

The City of Aurora, Department of Utilities originally wrote and compiled this book in 1980 with the help and support of many individuals and agencies. At the time of its publication, the book was one of the first guides to water conserving landscapes design available for Denver area residents.

The Aurora Water Conservation Office was also established in 1980. At that time, Aurora was one of the nation's fastest growing mid-sized cities and water conservation quickly became a very important aspect in water supply planning. Many innovative programs and activities have placed Aurora among the national leaders in water conservation programming. Today, water conservation continues to play a very important role to ensure adequate water for Aurora's future.

Since the compilation of the original book, a great deal of attention has been focused on water conserving landscapes. In 1980, the Denver Water Department coined the term "Xeriscape" as a systematic approach to landscaping for water conservation. Xeriscape, from the Greek word "xeri" for dry, has become synonymous with water conserving landscapes. Whether driven by drought, water supply limitations or a mere desire to have more efficient landscapes in our communities, the concept of water conserving landscapes has grown in popularity throughout the country.

Groups nationwide have worked to promote the concept of Xeriscape and water conservation. One such local group is Xeriscape Colorado! with membership representing the "green" industry, individuals, agencies and municipalities. Similar efforts throughout the country have lead to the creation of the National Xeriscape Council, Inc. For those interested in further information about the Council, contact the National Xeriscape Council, Inc., 940 East 51st St., Austin, Texas 78751.

Since the first writing of this book, many concepts and methods have changed or been improved indicating the need to update the material. **Landscaping for Water Conservation: Xeriscape** is primarily targeted to homeowners in the Denver/Aurora metro area. This book is written with the Front Range climate in mind, although the concepts are applicable in regions throughout the country.

Landscaping for Water Conservation: Xeriscape has been updated with the generous help of many area professionals. The Aurora Utilities Department would like to thank these professionals for their donation of time and expertise, and for making the update of this publication possible.

CONSULTANTS

PLANNING AND DESIGNING LANDSCAPES
Don Godi, Landscape Architect,
Donald Godi and Associates, Lakewood

Jim Knopf, Landscape Architect,
James Knopf and Associates, Boulder

John Stinson, Landscape Architect,
Colorado Design Group, Littleton

Anna Thurston, Landscape Designer-Architect,
Wild Iris Landscape Design and Consultation

GRASSES
Dorothy Borland, The Turf Expert, Denver

Gary Finstad, District Conservationist,
U.S. Soil Conservation Service

Paul Flack, Hydrologist, Aurora Utilities Department

PLANTS
Jim Borland, Flora West, Denver

Anna Thurston, Landscape Designer-Architect,
Wild Iris Landscape Design and Consultation

Larry Watson, Horticulture Consultant, Golden

Sally White, Morrison

SOIL AND SOIL IMPROVEMENT
Gary Finstad, District Conservationist,
U.S. Soil Conservation Service

Paul Flack, Hydrologist, Aurora Utilities Department

M. Bruce McCullough, State Soil Scientist,
U.S. Soil Conservation Service

PROPER IRRIGATION
Larry Keesen, Irrigation Consultant

John Stinson, Landscape Architect,
Colorado Design Group, Englewood

PHOTOGRAPHS
City of Aurora, Forestry Division

Denver Water Department

Ken Ball

James Knopf, Landscape Architect, Boulder

Alan Rollinger, Landscape Designer, Alan
Rollinger Landscapes, Denver

SKETCHES
Mike Lee, Associate Planner—Landscape Architect
City of Arvada

OVERALL
Ken Ball, Conservation Specialist,
Denver Water Department

Linda Clohessey, Drafter, Aurora Utilities Department

Dr. James Feucht, Professor-Landscape Plants,
Extension Landscape Plant Specialist, Colorado State
University Cooperative Extension

Gary Finstad, District Conservationist, U.S. Department
of Agriculture, U.S. Soil Conservation Service

Kim Hout, Water Conservation Specialist,
Aurora Utilities Department

Anna Thurston, Landscape Architect, Wild Iris

EDITING
Kimberley M. Knox, Water Conservation Technician,
Aurora Utilities Department

The book was printed in cooperation with Metro Water
Conservation, Inc.

Table of Contents

Introduction

Green areas have always played an important role in our lives and culture. The first town and city dwellers established common green areas in the middle of their towns. Later, modern city planners began designing parks and greenbelts throughout neighborhoods and business centers. We are drawn to green areas for their beauty and relaxing qualities. Even our homes reflect this need for green space. Real estate estimators have estimated that 20-30% of the value of an average home can be directly attributed to landscaping.

But before the settlers came to this region, the metro area was only a short-grass prairie with a few trees along the rivers. Since Aurora and surrounding cities only receive 14″ of precipitation in an average year, the plants that originally thrived in this grassland were known for their hardiness and drought-tolerance.

As settlers began to shape the area into a thriving city, they created large green lawns that reflected more of the area that they left in the eastern states and less of the semi-arid Front Range. Homeowners began to landscape their homes with high-water requiring turf areas, trees, shrubs and flowers. Unfortunately, these plants required supplemental water, and the metro area's water demand began to increase. In fact, recent studies have shown that about 50% of the water used in the metro area, is devoted to irrigating landscaped areas.

There is perhaps confusion that water is a plentiful, renewable resource. In arid and semi-arid regions, water is a frequently renewable but often limited resource. In Colorado, about 90 million acre-feet of precipitation falls each year. An acre-foot is the amount of water required to cover one acre of land to a depth of one foot. or 325,863 gallons. This sounds like a great deal, but on the average Colorado's streams only carry 16 million acre-feet of runoff. The majority of this precipitation evaporates, is used by vegetation, or percolates into the ground. Interstate compacts apportion slightly over half of the runoff to other states.

Over the years, the vast majority of Coloradoans have made their home on the Front Range. Since the climate of the metro area is semi-arid, limited amounts of surface and groundwater are available for use. Consequently, municipalities have invested in expensive water storage and conveyance systems to bring water from distant areas to the populated service areas. As an example, Aurora transports some water 180 miles over the continental divide in order to supply the water needs of its citizens.

As our population in Colorado and other western states increase, there will be increasing demands placed on the existing water supplies. We will experience greater limitations with our water resources as competing interests volley for ownership and use. However, using existing water supplies, our urban environment can be designed with landscapes which will only require a fraction of the water of traditional landscapes and will also have a better chance to withstand drought.

1

Why Landscaping for Water Conservation

Since outdoor water use represents approximately 50% of the water used in the metro area, a considerable amount of water can be saved through a well-planned and well-managed landscape. Yet, substantially reducing the amount of water used in landscape does not mean diminishing the beauty of the landscape. In fact, using less water usually translates into fewer disease problems, insect problems and maintenance needs. But the most important reason for landscaping for water conservation is to conserve and save Colorado's most precious natural resource, water.

This book is intended to help the reader create a beautiful, low-water requiring lawn that conserves water and creates an exciting and personally rewarding landscape. The goal of this publication is to give each reader the tools to create a landscape which fits his/her own needs, his/her home's environment, soil, climate and precipitation level.

Climate Metro Denver Area

The Denver metro area only receives 14" of natural precipitation in an average year. Most of this annual precipitation comes in heavy downpours in April and May. Due to the intensity of the storms, most of the water runs off rather than soaking into the soil. Another source of moisture are the heavy, limb-breaking snows. These storms usually come in the fall when leaves are still on the trees or in the late spring after the leaves have appeared and can cause damage to trees and shrubs.

During the summer and winter, it's not unusual to experience long dry spells with relatively low humidity readings. These spells combined with strong winter and spring winds, can dry and stress landscape plants.

The metro area also experiences great temperature variations. Summer temperatures are often above 90F, while winters will fluctuate between mild spells of 50F to minus 20F. Great variation between day and night are also the rule, with night temperatures often 40 degrees cooler than daytime highs.

Climate has a direct relation to the soils of the metro area. Due to our lack of precipitation, the soil tends to be alkaline without a great deal of organic matter. The lack of organic matter then creates a heavy soil that does not allow water to be easily absorbed. This can create water runoff and penetration problems.

Drought-Tolerant, Yet Beautiful Plants

To learn from the environment is to look at the enduring native plants, such as sumac, chokecherry, currant, sage, snow-on-the mountain, rabbitbush, buffalo and blue grama grasses. These plants thrived because they were adapted to the climate and the soils of the Front Range. Yet, they were beautiful enough to beckon the settlers to settle and thrive here as well.

There are also many adapted plants which fit the area's soil and precipitation conditions. These include hardy iceplant, iris, penstemon, gayfeather and tall fescue grass to name a few. These plants are beautiful and may lend beauty to any landscaped area.

Most of the plants now growing in landscapes along the Front Range are ill-suited to our area. They need maintenance, water and tender care in order to survive the area's climate, soils and precipitation. This in turn, creates an artificial environment with supplemental water needed to grow these exotic trees, shrubs, perennials and grasses that people have become accustomed to.

To create a landscape that is compatible with the climate of the Front Range, choose native and adapted low-water requiring plants that can easily fit into a beautiful landscape yet survive under extreme climate and soil conditions. Learn to maintain and care for these plants, so limited water is sufficient to keep them thriving even in the driest of times.

Creating a Beautiful, Low-Water Requiring Landscape

The step-by-step process of creating a low-water requiring, yet beautiful landscape has been best defined in the systematic approach of Xeriscape. Xeriscape, water conservation through creative landscaping, uses seven simple landscape principles. Depending on the landscape and the use of these principles, water savings from 30 to 80 percent have been obtained with the use of Xeriscape. The seven steps are:

— Planning and Design
— Limited Turf Areas
— Efficient Irrigation
— Soil Improvement
— Use Mulches
— Use Low-Water Demanding Plants
— Appropriate Maintenance

In the following chapters, each step will be discussed in further detail. Before beginning a landscape project, it may be best to read this book in its entirety.

Planning and Designing a Beautiful Landscape

Every successful project, including a landscape, needs to begin with a plan. In the process of developing a low water-using landscape or a Xeriscape, planning and design are critical elements. A landscape design should be developed to suit homeowners' needs, life styles and climate. A well-designed landscape plan can increase the value of the home as well as save water.

A homeowner moving into a new home without any landscaping can easily get caught in the trap of wanting to do something quickly. Children tracking in mud, dirt blowing onto new carpets and erosion problems can be very annoying. Unfortunately, quick solutions are not always the best solutions.

But by taking a little time and planning the landscape, the beauty of the entire home will be enhanced. Let's compare two landscapes. One uses a collection of unrelated trees and shrubs, while the other shows a creative, well-planned design. Both cost the same amount of money to install, yet the well-planned landscape can increase the value of the home. The disorderly landscape tends to decrease the value of the home. When it's time to maintain the landscape, the disorderly landscape will require more care, more

watering, more labor and more expense. The well-planned design with grouped plantings, can be more efficiently irrigated, reduce the amount of maintenance needed by using mulch beds and groundcovers, and allow the homeowners to have more time to enjoy their landscape instead of maintaining it.

To create a beautiful Xeriscape, the planning should include the step-by-step process and some key activities. For example, improving the soil and grading should be done prior to planting or seeding. To develop a well-planned design, homeowners have two options: have the plan professionally designed or do their own design. Money can be well spent to secure the advice of a competent landscape architect, landscape designer or a trained horticulturist who is well-versed in Xeriscape, in order to incorporate all the desirable features into a plan to fit particular needs and circumstances. The American Society of Landscape Architects-Colorado Chapter can offer referrals of landscape architects that can work within a specific budget and task. Others may wish to create their own design. But in either case, ideas about creating Xeriscape should be collected before beginning the project. Here are some avenues to get help.

— Read landscape-related books like this one, created and written for the area's particular climate.

— Attend seminars offered by local agencies.

— Visit nurseries and talk to qualified nursery representatives.

— Look at other yards and pick out certain design features that appeal to the eye.

— Visit Xeriscape demonstration gardens in the area.

— Call the local county Colorado State University Extension Office. The extension service is primarily responsible for extending Colorado State University education resources beyond the campus. They are able to provide unbiased information about the selection, planting and care of plant material in Colorado. Consult the blue pages under county government for the address and phone number of the local county Colorado State University Cooperative Extension Office.

Landscape Plans

Whether starting fresh on a Xeriscape or redoing an existing landscape, homeowners should follow these stages to create a design that will shape the landscape to their needs and ideas. Those three stages are:

— Site Analysis

— Use Analysis

— Site Plan Development

SITE ANALYSIS

The site analysis consists of an inventory and analysis of all existing features that may influence the landscape design. Carefully survey the lot. Using graph paper, draw a diagram of the lot. Get the dimensions of the lot from a copy of the site plan or actual dimensions. Draw the house onto the graph paper. Note on the map:

1. Direction of the prevailing winds

2. The location of south, north, east and west

3. Sunny and shady areas

4. Slopes and swales

5. Drainage areas

6. Existing Features
   a) Utilities
   b) Trees and Shrubs
   c) Walkways
   d) Existing Structures, i.e. fences, garages, patios and sheds

7. Attractive and not-so attractive views

City Requirements

Check to see if the city has any requirements on landscaping, fencing or trees. The city of Aurora does have a landscape ordinance which requires that all homeowners get a lawn permit. The permit requires the homeowners to show proof of proper soil preparation as defined by the ordinance. The city code requires that a minimum of three cubic yards of organic matter and ten lbs. of treble super phosphate per 1,000 sq. ft. be rototilled or disced in to a minimum depth of six inches. There is also a limit on the amount of high water-requiring turf that a homeowner may install as lawn. This amount is dependent on the total size of the lot. For more information about the Aurora Lawn Ordinance, call 695-7381 or stop by 1470 South Havana, Aurora, 80012.

USE ANALYSIS

The use analysis process of creating a Xeriscape or any type of landscape project consists of identifying the typical functions that a homeowner wants from his/her landscape. By doing a thorough use analysis before the site development phase, specific landscape materials (stone, wood, mulch, paving, turf, trees and shrubs) that help conserve water can be selected. Consider these ideas when working on the use analysis:

— Decide the overall theme of the landscape. It should work with the theme of the house's exterior and the neighborhood.

— Note any future building projects or additions planned for the site.

— Draw the traffic patterns, play areas, garbage dumpster or service areas and the entrance ways. The most durable plant for traffic is still turf grass. But since this plant requires the most irrigation (up to 25" in an average year), limit the turf to only traffic and play areas. For ease of maintenance, turf areas should not be obstructed by any plantings in the middle.

— Locate the garden area.

— Will any space be needed for a utility shed or storage area?

— Would the family enjoy a patio or deck?

Here are some tips on locating landscape materials:

— Locate bluegrass turf in high activity areas. Consider mulches, hard surfaces and low-water alternative landscapes in side yards and non-activity areas.

— Consider paving, gravel areas, etc. for walkways, entry areas and seating areas.

Site Analysis

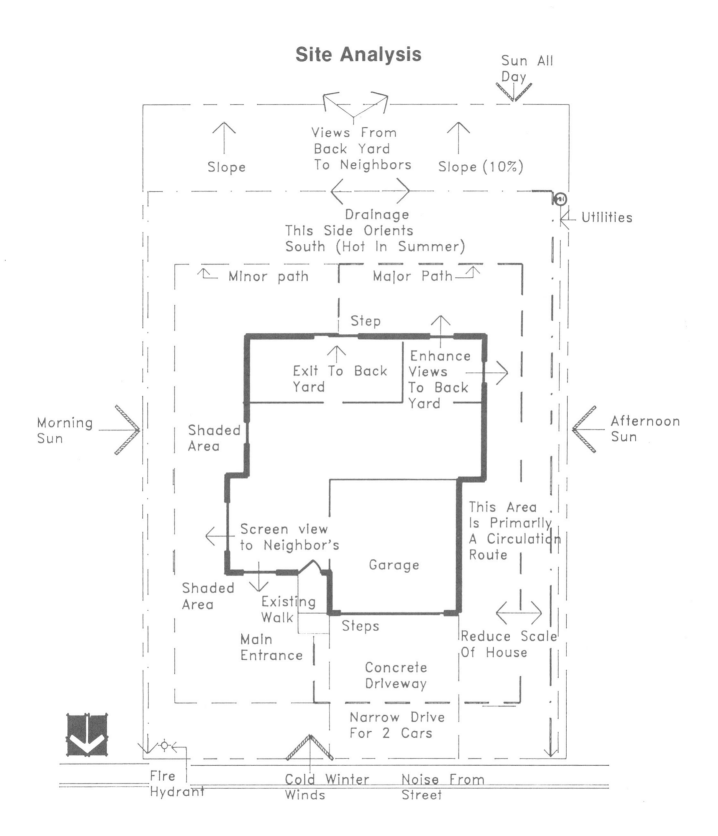

Sun All Day

Views From Back Yard To Neighbors

Slope

Slope (10%)

Utilities

Drainage
This Side Orients
South (Hot In Summer)

Minor path

Major Path

Step

Exit To Back Yard

Enhance Views To Back Yard

Morning Sun

Afternoon Sun

Shaded Area

This Area Is Primarily A Circulation Route

Screen view to Neighbor's

Garage

Shaded Area

Existing Walk

Reduce Scale Of House

Main Entrance

Steps

Concrete Driveway

Narrow Drive For 2 Cars

Fire Hydrant

Cold Winter Winds

Noise From Street

Use Analysis

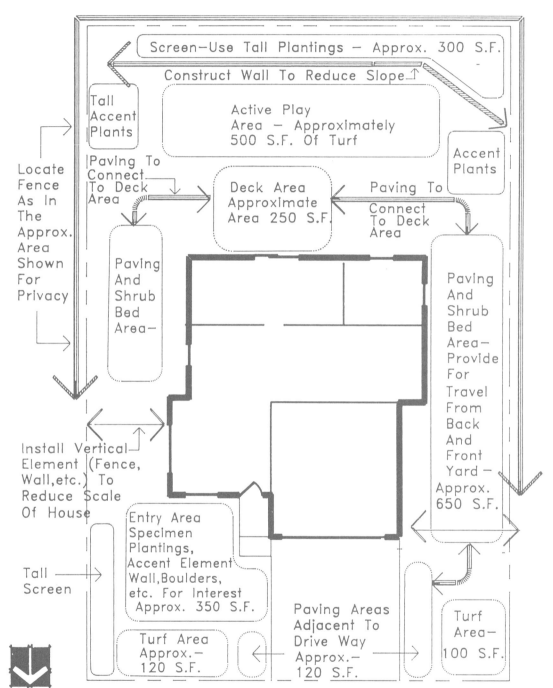

Screen—Use Tall Plantings — Approx. 300 S.F.

Construct Wall To Reduce Slope

Tall Accent Plants

Active Play Area — Approximately 500 S.F. Of Turf

Accent Plants

Locate Fence As In The Approx. Area Shown For Privacy

Paving To Connect To Deck Area

Deck Area Approximate Area 250 S.F.

Paving To Connect To Deck Area

Paving And Shrub Bed Area—

Paving And Shrub Bed Area— Provide For Travel From Back And Front Yard — Approx. 650 S.F.

Install Vertical Element (Fence, Wall,etc.) To Reduce Scale Of House

Tall Screen

Entry Area Specimen Plantings, Accent Element Wall,Boulders, etc. For Interest Approx. 350 S.F.

Turf Area Approx.— 120 S.F.

Paving Areas Adjacent To Drive Way Approx.— 120 S.F.

Turf Area— 100 S.F.

Note: S.F. Is An Abbreviation For Square Feet

6

- Pay attention to outside view from inside the house. Don't block the views with large shrubs and trees.

- Use fencing, large shrubs and trees to screen objectionable views.

- Locate plants in areas where they would get the sunlight and moisture that they need in order to survive and grow.

- Address problem areas like swales or hills. With areas that receive a lot of water like drainage ways, plants that require a lot of water are a good choice.

- Elevated or hilly areas should have a groundcover or any spreading plant that keeps soil erosion down, but doesn't require mowing.

- Locate shrub beds away from the house's foundation where they can be viewed from interior windows. Frequent watering of shrub beds may cause damage to building foundations.

- Use large deciduous trees to provide summer shade.

- Plant evergreens to block objectionable views, lessen winter winds and for privacy.

- Native rock walls, boulders and low-mass shrub plantings are effective ways to moderate and stabilize slopes.

- Locate plants and space them according to their full maturity width and height. Avoid planting them too close to each other, buildings and utility lines.

SITE PLAN DEVELOPMENT

Once the overall plan has been determined, list the goals for this season and future seasons. This allows the entire project to be completed as time and funds allow. Remember Rome wasn't built in a day nor on a one-year budget! Take time to enjoy the Xeriscape project and avoid costly and timely mistakes.

- Make necessary grade changes first. Be sure that water flows away from the house.

- Lay out and install irrigation systems before plants are installed. Be sure to group plants with similar water needs together to avoid water waste and reduce maintenance.

- Try to finish the hard-surface areas before planting lawns and shrubs.

- Mature shade trees are the single most valuable item in the landscape. They should be among the first plants installed in the first season.

- Proper soil preparation is crucial to all plants. Before installing any plant material, it's best to have the soil analyzed. Contact the local county CSU Cooperative Extension Office for details about a soil test.

- Place large boulders and other features before placing plants.

- Reduce turf areas to only where it is absolutely necessary, such as high traffic areas.

- Placing mulch around new turf gives the project a finished appearance. Planting in mulch areas can take place on a regular basis over the next few years. The mulch will help retain moisture for the plants and will help reduce weed growth.

Design Elements

There is a wide variety of landscape materials and options that can be used in a Xeriscape. Below is an overview of the more commonly-used options and their advantages and disadvantages in a water-conserving landscape.

1. PLANT MATERIALS

Plant materials are usually the first consideration in a landscape design. They can be used:

- As architectural elements to define outdoor rooms such as trees for ceilings or canopies and shrubs as walls, and to direct or block views

- For environmental control or erosion, acoustics, foot traffic, glare and reflection

- For climate control such as wind, sun and temperature

- For visual interest and the creation of sound and odors

- For the provision of food and cover for birds and other animals

Trees

The use of trees can achieve several effects.

- A tree's shade will lower the air and soil temperature. In fact, air temperature may be reduced as much as 12° to 20°F. This in turn reduces the moisture loss of the nearby plants.

- Trees can form windbreaks to reduce the wind velocity and thereby reduce the moisture loss from nearby plants and surrounding soil. Consider placing large deciduous trees on south and southwest quadrants of the property, in order to provide shade on outdoor decks and patios.

- Trees can create screens for undesirable sights and sounds.

Site Plan Development

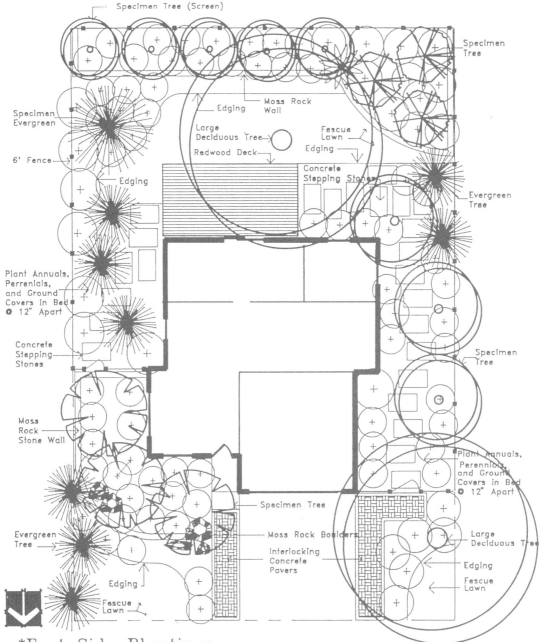

Specimen Tree (Screen)

Specimen Tree

Specimen Evergreen

6' Fence

Edging

Edging

Moss Rock Wall

Large Deciduous Tree

Redwood Deck

Fescue Lawn

Edging

Concrete Stepping Stones

Evergreen Tree

Plant Annuals, Perrenials, and Ground Covers in Bed @ 12" Apart

Concrete Stepping Stones

Specimen Tree

Moss Rock Stone Wall

Plant Annuals, Perennials, and Ground Covers in Bed @ 12" Apart

Evergreen Tree

Edging

Fescue Lawn

Specimen Tree

Moss Rock Boulders

Interlocking Concrete Pavers

Large Deciduous Tree

Edging

Fescue Lawn

*East Side Plantings
*Soil Amendments
*Stepping Stones
*Plant Shrubs
*Plant Perennials And Ground Covers
*Edging
*Irrigation Addition

*Finish Small Shrub Beds In Front And Back Yards
*Soil Amendments
*Spread Mulch
*Plant Shrubs
*Irrigation Addition
*Edging

— They define overhead space or create a "room" effect.

— Trees can be used to lend different seasonal colors and textures throughout the year.

— Trees can create a focal point as specimen trees.

— Evergreens in a mass planting can create screens and backdrops by displaying ornamental trees and flowers.

— Small deciduous trees are useful as accents. Hardy flowering varieties such as Hawthornes, Plums and Golden Raintrees and some species of Crabapples work well in highly visible areas such as the entrance way, adjacent to patio areas or areas visible from the interior windows.

— Mixing drought-tolerant species such as Russian Olives and Bigtooth Maples that have interesting foliage with evergreens produce striking results.

— Deep-rooted trees such as Hackberry and Kentucky Coffeetree, take less moisture from soil surface, i.e. less competition with shallow-rooted trees however can not put their roots in soils that are tightly compacted, have restrictive layers or have lack of air.

Scale is very important. Choose locations where trees will have room to develop to their full mature size. This then provides appropriate scale to house and property size. Trees come in various shapes and sizes.

Shrubs

There is a wide variety of drought-tolerant shrubs for residential landscapes. Shrubs exist in all shapes, colors, sizes and textures. As with any plant, shrubs need to be grouped according to water and exposure needs. Groupings will reduce water and maintenance needs. Another maintenance tip with shrubs is to mulch heavily around the shrub's trunk to an optimal three-inch to 4-inch depth.

— Taller shrubs planted in masses can be used as backdrops. Some taller shrubs are native oak, sand cherry, Russian sage and staghorn sumac.

— Shrubs can also be used as an accent or provide foregound colors. Spirea, potentillas and cranberry cotoneasters are only a few of the shrubs that can provide color.

— They can be used effectively in combination with trees as windbreaks, i.e. shrubs will slow down wind passing under trees. (Sketch 1)

— Shrubs may create "visual weight" to a landscape.

Shrubs can also add color and texture, can serve as screens, attract birds and other wildlife, define space, and provide shade to the soil surface.

Dense planting of conifers and shrubs to intercept and break up strong wind flow currents.

Leeward side with wind speed reduction for a distance of approximately 10 times the height of windbreak.

Windward side with maximum wind velocity.

Sketch 1. Windbreaks

Living Groundcovers

An effective groundcover plant covers a relatively large area by spreading. Certain groundcovers will form a dense mat or cover which limits the amount of sunlight that will penetrate the ground surface and discourage weed growth. If drought-tolerant species are selected, these types of groundcovers may be used as a substitute for turfgrass. These low-water requiring groundcovers may use much less water and require less maintenance than a bluegrass yard.

Groundcovers can be used for a variety of purposes: reducing soil erosion, creating a carpet effect and acting as an attractive design feature. There is a wide variety of deciduous and evergreen groundcovers that are low-water requiring and very hardy.

— Groundcovers can be used in place of turf especially on steep banks, exposed hot banks, and to trap and retain snow.

— They can create a low-maintenance, beautiful alternative for non-traffic areas such as side yards and narrow strips.

— Flowering groundcovers may be used as wildflowers.

— Use edging material between turf and groundcover areas, to prevent grass from invading groundcover plantings.

Grasses

This is the most common landscape option. Yet, it can be one of the most maintenance-intensive and water-requiring options.

— Grass may be used for high traffic areas, such as playgrounds and sports fields.

— Low-water requiring grasses may be used to create a meadow-like effect.

Vines

Vines may also be used as groundcover or as a shade element over a screen or trellis.

— Vines can be used as a softening element on structures.

— They may be used for seasonal color. Some are evergreen, while others produce an intense fall color.

— They can be an element of fine tracery on fences and walls.

Annual and Perennial Flowers

There is a wide variety of low-water requiring annual and perennial flowers. Annuals only last one growing season, while perennials keep coming back year after year.

— Flowers may be used as elements of seasonal color. When used in shrub or groundcover beds, place flowers on inside curves of bed lines to create a professional look.

— Blue colors in the background dramatize depth.

— Flowers can be placed in different locations in planters and hanging baskets to create a different visual effect or accent.

Vegetable/Fruits

Vegetable gardens can also be a creative part of the landscape. They don't necessarily have to be rectangular or square. If flower or groundcover beds are carved out in the backyard, follow the bed lines for vegetable gardens. Fruit trees can serve a double purpose. They can also provide the effect of an ornamental or canopy tree, and at the same time provide food. They also create high productivity in a limited area.

2. STRUCTURES

Fences

Before building a fence, check with the city's regulations on height and visibility. Both fences and retaining walls should be constructed to compliment the texture, material, complexity and detailing of the site's main structure.

— Fences may define space, screen out undesirable views and noises, reduce wind velocity and produce ground shade.

— Fences may be used to insure privacy.

— Fences can provide support for vines and provide a back drop for flowers, shrubs and small trees.

— Be sure that the fence blends in with the landscape.

— Be aware that your fences will create areas of micro-climates

— The fence design should be planned to withstand high winds.

— Fences can be used as a partition to segment various activites in your landscape.

— Wood may add a natural warmth to the design.

Retaining Walls

Retaining walls can be built with a variety of materials, including stone. Much of the same uses of a fence are applicable to a retaining wall.

— Retaining walls may be used to create terraces and other level spaces.

— They may be used to moderate slopes and slow water runoff.

— They may be softened by cascading plant material.

— A wide variety of stone materials are available.

— Retaining walls can be used to create an illusion of depth or to create physical partitions in the landscape.

Overhead Structures

These structures such as gazebos and patios, create a permanent element in the landscape. They can be built as a solid or vented unit.

— Overhead structures may provide shade.

— They may provide support for vines and hanging planters.

— They may provide a sense of enclosure.

— Construction should compliment the dominant structure of the landscape (usually the house).

Surfaces

These include pavements and decks that provide almost year-round enjoyment of a landscape. They also reduce the area that needs to be watered.

— Surfaces can define areas of intense activity and circulation, and can also be used in seating areas.

— Avoid using pavement such as concrete or brick on a sunny or south side of the house. Otherwise, the heat will reflect into the living quarters.

— Plant deciduous trees and shrubs within the paved areas, if pavement is to be used as a passive solar element. This diffuses the pavement's reflected heat in the summer.

— Light-colored pavements will create glare.

— Paving materials come in a wide variety of shapes, colors and textures.

— Avoid large continuous expanses of paving or long uninterrupted straight edges.

Buildings

See "fences, walls," etc.

— When choosing plants to be used adjacent to buildings, consider wind and sun exposure and resultant soil moisture conditions, reflected heat, roof overhangs, etc.

— Be sure to consider the views from inside and outside the house.

Sculptures

These visual features will compliment walls, drive, sidewalks, courtyards, water features, rock gardens or lawn areas. They may provide a touch of culture and uniqueness to the landscape.

3. MULCHES

Mulches serve to unify a landscape design. An example might be using cedar bark or shavings with its distinctive red color as a mulch or a top dressing in all of the planting beds. Mulches can be organic, such as wood chips or bark or inorganic, such as rock and gravel. Both serve an important function in a landscape.

All mulches modify the extremes of soil temperature and organic mulches increase the fertility of the soil. A 3" to 4" depth is normally optimum. Depending on the mulch and growing conditions, a depth deeper than 5" will discourage plants from growing and create an obstacle for water to get down to the soil. Mulches are covered in depth in Chapter 5.

4. IRRIGATION

The design of irrigation systems is extremely important in developing water-conserving landscapes. An effective irrigation system can increase water savings in a well-designed landscape. A poorly designed irrigation system can actually increase water consumption and waste.

In order to avoid waste, the plants with similar water needs should be grouped together. The irrigation system should then be designed to deliver the amount of water that each grouping needs to be healthy and vigorous. All plants, including Xeric, need some sort of irrigation system in order to become established. Irrigation is addressed in Chapter 3.

5. GRADING/CONTOURING

Grading modifications are critical in creating an exciting and functional landscape. The grading plan should be developed carefully as a part of the overall landscape design. Since grading is the first major step, grading mistakes are difficult to resolve after a landscape project has been completed.

Grading and contouring has a profound effect upon the visual and functional quality of a landscape. Grading is critical for proper drainage to ensure that water does not damage existing structures or paving. Proper drainage is also important to the health of the plant. Some plants like moist conditions, but most plants can not survive in a sustained wet environment.

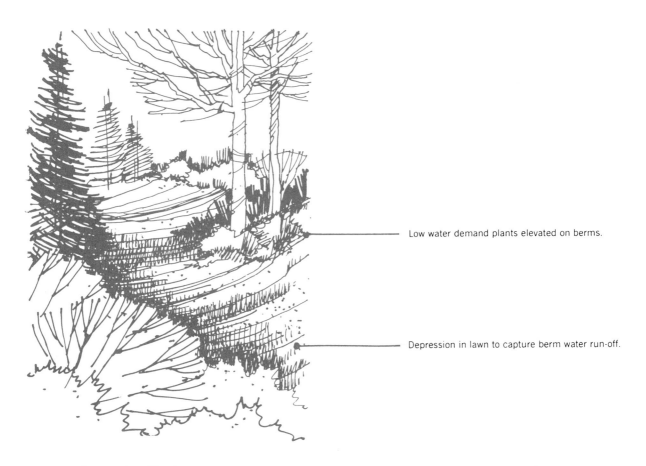

Low water demand plants elevated on berms.

Depression in lawn to capture berm water run-off.

Sketch 2. Depressions/Swales

Landform Changes

A landform change can be a creation of slope, small hill or a berm. Landscape architects prefer that landform changes be to scale with the site or in other words, a gradual rather than an abrupt change. If the homeowner prefers an abrupt change, the berm should contain other structural applications like rock boulders, walls, etc.

— The incline of a slope or berm should not exceed 4:1.

— Berms/slopes provide relief to a flat surface.

— Berms/slopes should be constructed with smooth transition, so it is not lumpy or have a grave-like appearance.

— If the design calls for a formal effect, only then plant the trees directly on top of the berm.

— Berms define space, add interest and may be used to divert water and retain water (as dams).

— Berms should not be used for screening purposes since they can not be built high enough to screen any noise or view.

— Berms or mounds direct moisture outward, while depressions hold moisture and in some cases, trap moisture.

— Plants along the edge are recommended to utilize the available moisture.

— If the design calls for a steep slope, it is best to use terraces. Terracing will eliminate a lot of water runoff problems.

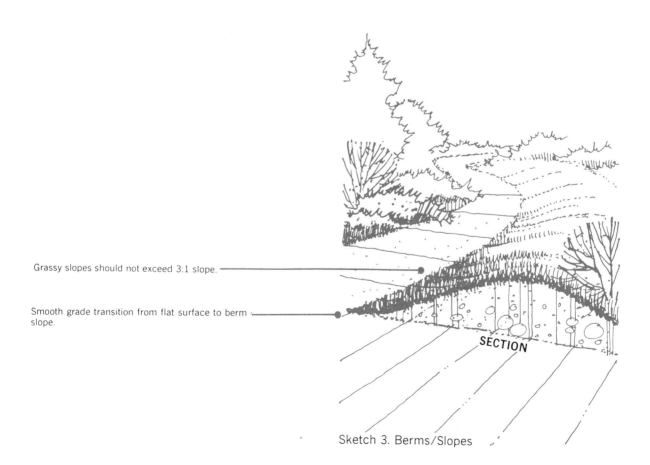

Grassy slopes should not exceed 3:1 slope.

Smooth grade transition from flat surface to berm slope.

SECTION

Sketch 3. Berms/Slopes

Depressions/Swales

Depressions and swales help maximize the use of the natural precipitation or rainfall. They can be tree wells or depressions around high-water demand areas. Water from gutters or drainage pipes can also be channeled to high-water requiring plant areas.

— Use caution when working with depressions or swales. If water is standing for a long period of time, it may sour the soil and cause oxygen starvation. Make sure that the swales are not going to cause any flooding problems to the landscape, the home or even homes that are downstream from the swale.

— It is best to use a restricted drain outlet to release the stored water at a slower rate. This will then allow the water to have a chance to soak into the soil, before it runs off the soil surface.

— Depressions can be used to define space in outdoor living areas.

— Swales and depressions can also be used to capture and hold snow away from traffic areas like driveways or sidewalks.

— Long swales can raise the immediate area's water table.

— Locating plants slightly elevated but adjacent to swales or depressions ensures positive drainage for the plants.

6. SOIL

Improving soil is an important step in the Xeriscape process to develop a low water-requiring landscape. Soil and soil improvements are covered in detail in Chapter 4.

7. LIGHTING

This is an important and creative landscape component, but it does not deal directly with water conservation. Nursery men and landscape architects can best give you the latest details and trends in this exciting area of landscape.

8. WATER FEATURES

Water features can play an important role in a landscape. By incorporating water features, micro-climates with higher humidity can be created. In turn, this gives the illusion of a different climate within the metro area's dry, hot climate.

— Municipalities may have zoning regulations on water features. To get zoning information for the City of Aurora, contact the Code Enforcement Office at 695-7365.

— To minimize the amount of water needed, be sure to contain the water feature in a small, recirculating system. To further minimize the loss of water due to evaporation, use evaporation retardents.

— Don't create a water feature that is so deep, that it can cause a hazard for small children or animals.

— Avoid overdoing a water feature to the point that it dominates the landscape. By using the water feature to compliment (rather than dominate) a landscape, the landscape can lend a more pleasing affect.

Designs For All Sorts Of Homes

So how can all of these landscape components be used in a landscape design? How can challenges be addressed in a design? On the following pages, four demonstration plans are given. They are for an older home, a new cluster home, new single-family home and an older farmstead. These plans are to be used only as demonstrations, but they are also intended to illustrate the concept that thoughtful landscape planning can increase the value of the property and still reduce water consumption.

The following designs should be viewed with a master planning approach. Once a homeowner's plan is established, the priorities and phases of the landscape development can then be set over several years and several budgets. In order to truly reduce costs, it is very important to first do certain key items, like installing irrigation systems or amending the soil. To help facilitate the scheduling of the project, a list of the construction sequence has been given with each design. Again, one should add their own needs and ideas about their home and landscape.

Illustration 1-1

NEW CLUSTER HOME

Lot Size 40′ by 75′ = 3000 sq. ft.

Family Members

- Adults-young, single
- Children-none
- Pets-none

Existing Conditions

- Home and garage positioned against side property line
- Direct access to common greenbelt landscape
- Privacy fences around courtyard area
- Concrete pad adjacent to kitchen
- No outward views from courtyard

Desires, Needs, Uses

- Private outdoor living space with good interior views
- Comfortable outdoor area
- Patio space convenient to kitchen
- Minimum maintenance and water requirement
- Water feature

Landscape Components

This cluster home illustrates the use of the following components and concepts:

- Fences to provide high degree of privacy and containment of views to inside of courtyard
- Variety of hard surfaces for intensive use areas
- Overhead structure for shade
- Large canopy of deciduous trees for summer shade and "ceiling effect"
- Lack of lawn area to reduce maintenance and conserve water
- Extensive plantings to create more comfortable outdoor room with good views
- Automatic irrigation system to reduce maintenance

Construction Sequence

- Fence
- Brick Paving and overhead structure
- Gravel walk
- Soil preparation in planting areas
- Irrigation System
- Shade trees and mulch
- Boulders
- Plantings and mulch
- Water feature
- Wood deck

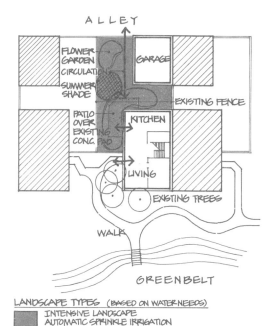

STUDY PLAN

Sketch A

0   20   NORTH

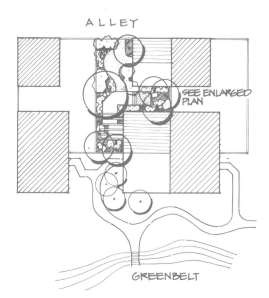

DESIGN PLAN

Sketch B

0   20   NORTH

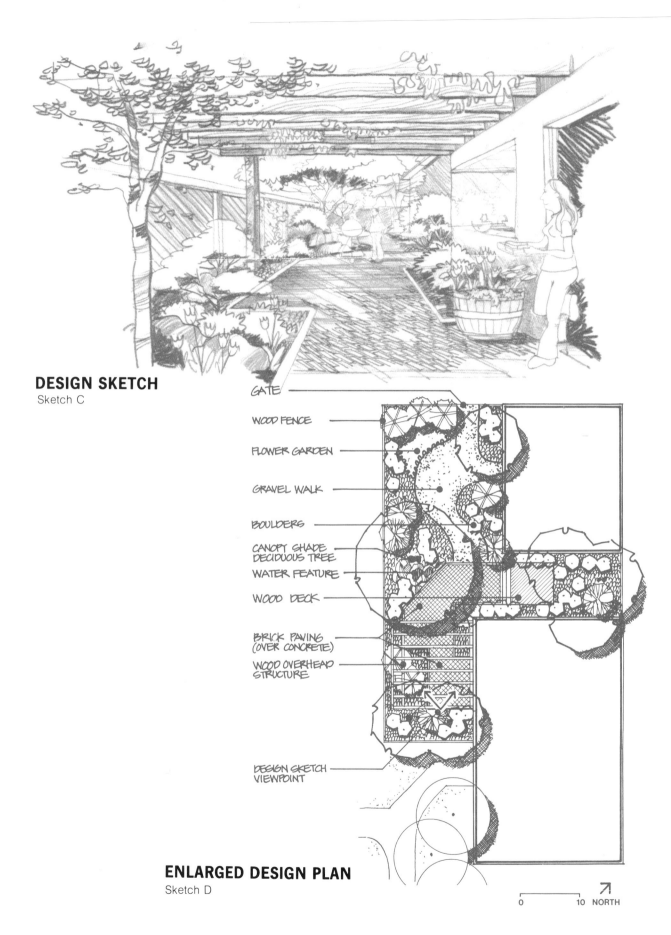

DESIGN SKETCH
Sketch C

GATE

WOOD FENCE

FLOWER GARDEN

GRAVEL WALK

BOULDERS

CANOPY SHADE
DECIDUOUS TREE

WATER FEATURE

WOOD DECK

BRICK PAVING
(OVER CONCRETE)

WOOD OVERHEAD
STRUCTURE

DESIGN SKETCH
VIEWPOINT

ENLARGED DESIGN PLAN
Sketch D

0   10   NORTH

Illustration 1-2

OLDER HOME

Lot Size: 50' x 125' = 6250 sq. ft.

Family Members

- Adults-young couple
- Children-none
- Pets-cat

Existing Conditions

- Home located on a terrace with detached garage
- Corner lot
- Small front and back yards
- Narrow sideyards
- Steep slope with hot, south exposure
- Large trees on adjacent street right-of-way and private property
- Narrow parkways
- Good protection from winds

Desires, Needs, Uses

- Private outdoor living space with good interior views
- Vegetable and fruit garden
- Flower garden
- Service area adjacent to alley
- Minimum maintenance and water requirement
- Active and passive outdoor use areas: cooking, eating, sitting, games

Landscape Components

The landscape of this older single family residence was renovated to make use of the following components and concepts:

- Remove existing walks to permit creation of lawn and deck areas
- Pavement and decking in high activity areas to reduce the amount of irrigated areas and to create more useful areas
- Remove unused lawn areas
- Planting beds to replace lawn, to reduce water requirement and maintenance
- Low-water requiring plants in parkway to replace lawn
- Large canopy of deciduous trees for summer shade
- Planting masses for privacy screening
- Flower bed as visual focal point

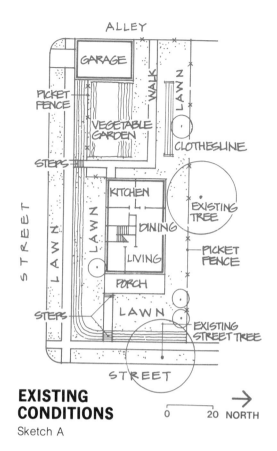

EXISTING CONDITIONS

0   20 NORTH

Sketch A

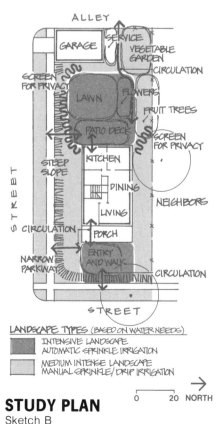

LANDSCAPE TYPES (BASED ON WATER NEEDS)

INTENSIVE LANDSCAPE AUTOMATIC SPRINKLE IRRIGATION

MEDIUM INTENSE LANDSCAPE MANUAL SPRINKLE/DRIP IRRIGATION

STUDY PLAN

0   20 NORTH

Sketch B

17

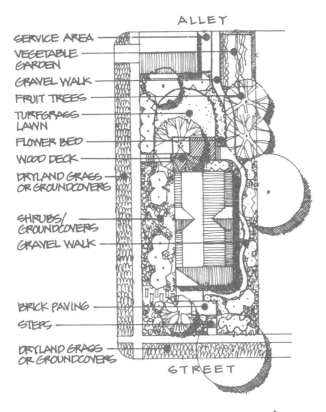

ALLEY

SERVICE AREA
VEGETABLE GARDEN
GRAVEL WALK
FRUIT TREES
TURFGRASS LAWN
FLOWER BED
WOOD DECK
DRYLAND GRASS OR GROUNDCOVERS
SHRUBS/ GROUNDCOVERS
GRAVEL WALK
BRICK PAVING
STEPS
DRYLAND GRASS OR GROUNDCOVERS

STREET

Construction Sequence

- Remove existing walks
- New wood deck
- New walk and steps
- Remove old lawn
- Soil preparation in planting areas
- Irrigation system
- New lawn
- Parkway plantings
- Plantings and mulch

DESIGN PLAN
Sketch C

0   20 NORTH →

EXISTING LANDSCAPE
Sketch D

NEW LANDSCAPE
Sketch E

DESIGN SKETCHES

18

Illustration 1-3

NEW SUBURBAN HOME

Lot Size 100' by 70' = 17,000 sq. ft.

Family Members

- Adults-couple in their 40's
- Children-2 toddlers
- Pets-dog

Existing Conditions

- Adjacent houses on three sides
- Site flat with poor drainage
- Large open front and back yards
- Narrow side streets
- Exposed to winds
- Steep, hot front area
- Bare subsoil (topsoil has been removed)
- No existing vegetation

Desires, Needs, Uses

- Open areas for entertainment and play
- Privacy for outdoor living areas
- Low maintenance and water requirement
- Service area at the side of the garage
- Play area for children
- Dog run area

Landscape Components

This suburban home landscape utilizes the following components and concepts:
- Hard surfaces for intensive active use areas
- Overhead structure for shade
- Dry creek bed to channel run-off water around home and active use areas; for visual interest, and to create an edge between differing landscape types
- Plantings along dry creek bed edge to utilize run off
- Lawn areas for active use areas such as play, games
- Dryland plantings for non-active use areas to reduce water requirement and maintenance
- Fence and plants as windbreaks to lessen impact of winds
- Fence, berms and plants for greater privacy
- Berms for good drainage and visual interest
- Irrigation system to reduce maintenance and for efficient distribution of water
- Play area for chidren located adjacent to lawn area in clear view of kitchen
- Large deciduous trees for shade

Construction Sequence

- Grading for berms, lawn, dry creek bed
- Patio, wood deck and overhead structure, walks
- Soil preparation in planting areas
- Dry creek bed
- Irrigation system
- Living ground covers-dryland grasses
- Windbreaks and mulch
- Dog run
- Fence
- Plantings and mulch
- Turf for play area

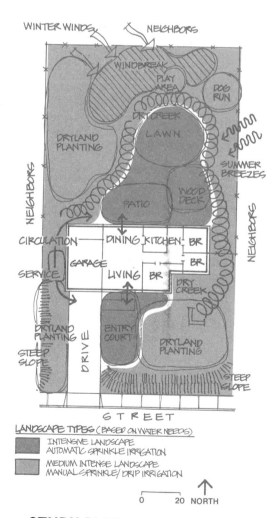

STUDY PLAN
Sketch A

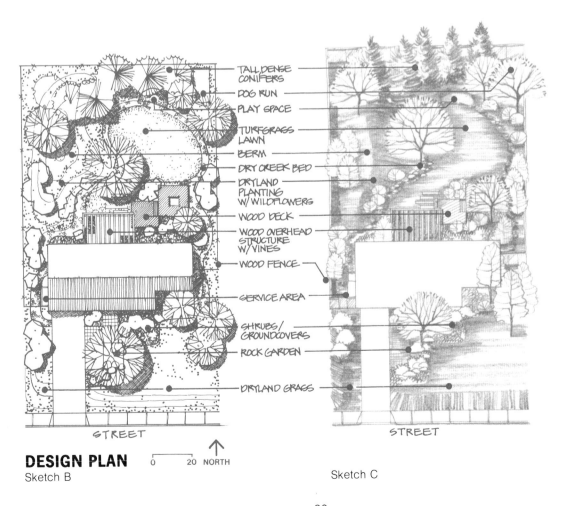

TALL DENSE CONIFERS

DOG RUN

PLAY SPACE

TURFGRASS LAWN

BERM

DRY CREEK BED

DRYLAND PLANTING W/WILDFLOWERS

WOOD DECK

WOOD OVERHEAD STRUCTURE W/VINES

WOOD FENCE

SERVICE AREA

SHRUBS/ GROUNDCOVERS

ROCK GARDEN

DRYLAND GRASS

STREET

STREET

DESIGN PLAN
Sketch B

0   20 NORTH

Sketch C

Illustration 1-4

OLDER FARMSTEAD

Lot size-several acres

Family Members

- Adults-couple in their 40's
- Children-3 teenagers
- Pets-dogs, cats, horses and chickens

Existing Conditions

- Detached garage and stable
- Very open and exposed to winds
- Panoramic views of mountains
- Large shade trees
- Intermittent creek adjacent to house
- Rock outcroppings
- Surrounding prairie landscape

Desire, Needs, Use

- Outdoor area for entertainment of large groups
- Maintain distant view of mountains
- Minimum amount of landscape requiring intensive watering and maintenance
- Blend intensive landscape use areas to dryland non-intense areas
- Protection from winter winds

Landscape Components

This older homestead makes use of the following concepts and components:

- Most intense landscape use areas adjacent to house
- Transition landscape between the outdoor intense activity area and the natural prairie
- Natural prairie landscape in outlying areas and covering the greatest amount of area
- Planting windbreaks to lessen the effect of winter winds
- Channelization of the summer breezes for cooling effect
- Retaining walls to eliminate steep slope to create level terrace for the outdoor activity area and to create an edge between differing landscape types
- Gravel surfaces for driveway and footpaths
- Irrigation system to reduce maintenance and for efficient distribution of water in areas around the residence

Construction Sequence

- Drives and footpaths
- Retaining wall and stone steps
- Soil preparation
- Irrigation system
- Living ground covers-lawn for active areas and dryland grass
- Windbreaks and mulch
- Plantings and mulch

ELEVATION/SECTION A-A

Sketch A

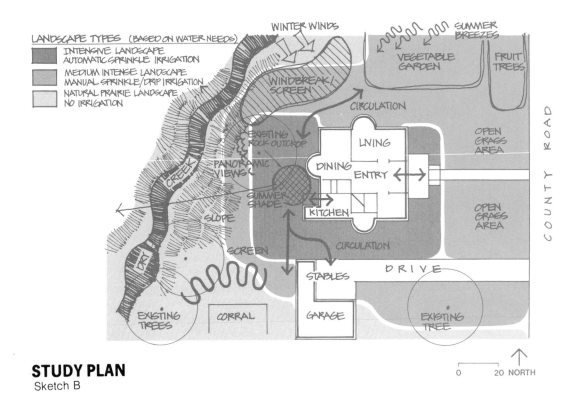

WINTER WINDS

SUMMER BREEZES

VEGETABLE GARDEN

FRUIT TREES

WINDBREAK/ SCREEN

CIRCULATION

EXISTING ROCK OUTCROP

PANORAMIC VIEWS

CREEK

SUMMER SHADE

SLOPE

SCREEN

DRY

EXISTING TREES

CORRAL

LIVING

DINING

ENTRY

KITCHEN

CIRCULATION

STABLES

DRIVE

GARAGE

OPEN GRASS AREA

OPEN GRASS AREA

EXISTING TREE

COUNTY ROAD

STUDY PLAN
Sketch B

0   20 NORTH

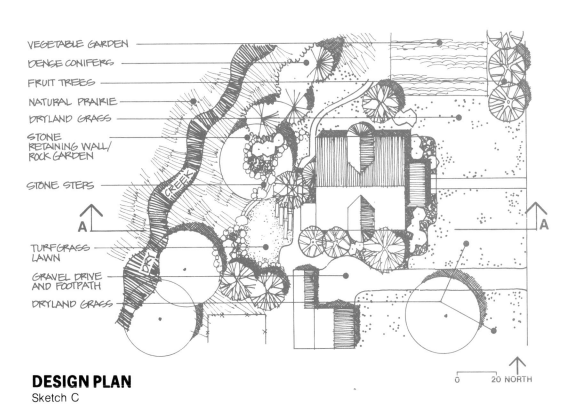

VEGETABLE GARDEN

DENSE CONIFERS

FRUIT TREES

NATURAL PRAIRIE

DRYLAND GRASS

STONE RETAINING WALL/ ROCK GARDEN

STONE STEPS

CREEK

DRY

A

A

TURFGRASS LAWN

GRAVEL DRIVE AND FOOTPATH

DRYLAND GRASS

DESIGN PLAN
Sketch C

0   20 NORTH

PERSPECTIVE ON LANDSCAPING AND LANDSCAPE DESIGN

Many of us seem to have a desire for highly irrigated landscapes and have forgotten the beauty of Colorado's semi-arid climate.

Many Denver metro homes have large expanses of irrigated and manicured lawns. They are matched with isolated planting beds of high-water requiring flowers which require a great deal of maintenance. A common sight on the weekends is to see the entire family weeding, watering and mowing the lawn.

Newcomers come from all over the country and often leave the natural lushness of areas with high precipitation. They do not realize that the Denver metro area only receives 14″ of precipitation in an average year. To make themselves more comfortable in their new homes, developers and they duplicate the lush landscapes of their hometowns. The annual green lawn contests have encouraged homeowners to create showcase lawns and gardens that have little or no relationship to Colorado's reality. Irrigated landscapes with the lush or English tradition have become models for residential projects, as well as commercial and industrial complexes.

Yet, Colorado has different beauty-a more subtle beauty of its own. This beauty has its own unique challenges. Let's go over some of the differences in Colorado from other states:

— Colorado experiences fluctuating weather conditions. Two consecutive days might have a 40 degree temperature difference.

— In the summer, Colorado's citizens enjoy warm days and cool nights.

— Colorado has a wide variety of geological features and natural, rugged landscapes.

— Colorado offers a seasonal variety with temperatures, colors and textures.

— There is an abundance of wildlife in Colorado.

— Colorado offers a wide variety of habitats-from prairies to forest and from streams to meadows.

All of this and more makes Colorado unique and exciting. More and more people are choosing to create landscapes using what Colorado has to offer, while at the same time conserve its most precious natural resource, water. This new style or idea of landscaping that has emerged is called XERISCAPE. Again, Xeriscape is a process or style using seven simple steps to create a beautiful, yet low-water requiring lawn.

This book is designed to give a homeowner tools to create his/her landscape with this exciting new process!

Grasses

When planning a Xeriscape, the step of "reducing turf area" is a key component in reducing water consumption in Front Range landscaping. Recent studies have estimated that 50% of the water consumed in the metro area, is spent on landscaping. The majority of this water is devoted to turfgrass areas.

Most of the Denver metro residential and commercial landscapes are primarily covered with Kentucky bluegrass. Kentucky bluegrass has many advantages. It is extremely traffic-hardy and drought-tolerant. But in order to maintain Kentucky bluegrass' famous deep green color, it may require up to 39″ of moisture in an average year. That is 25″ over the natural average precipitation in the Denver metro area. Studies have also shown that a majority of homeowners typically overwater their lawns. Kentucky bluegrass has its place in traffic areas, but many areas within a landscape can be addressed with low-water requiring alternative turfgrasses. For more information on proper irrigation, read Chapter 3. For more information on maintaining Kentucky bluegrass, read Chapter 7.

There are many interesting native and adapted grasses that can be used as low-water use alternatives to the traditional irrigated bluegrass lawn. Most of these grasses have a different texture and color than irrigated bluegrass, yet they can create a beautiful landscape. The selection of a grass, as with any other landscape plant, should be based on a landscape design. Landscapes should serve the needs of the homeowner and alternative grasses should be selected based on how well they fit the needs of the design and plan.

DESIGN ASPECTS WITH ALTERNATIVE TURF GRASSES

Grasses vary widely in physical appearance, growth habit and management requirements. Before selecting a grass species, one should consider these points:

1. What is the purpose of the grass? Is the grass going to be essentially a groundcover for a large area? Does it need to have a manicured look? Is the turf going to be used as an ornamental border or a mass planting?

2. What kind of soil does the area have? Is it clayey or sandy?

3. Is the planting area sunny or shady?

4. How much irrigation is planned after the turf has been established?

DIFFERENCES BETWEEN TURF AND GRASSES

Homeowners should be aware of two distinctions with turfgrasses. There are warm-season grasses and cool-season grasses. Warm-season grasses make seed and grow during the warm days of summer. They do not turn green until the middle of spring and will go dormant and turn beige in late summer/early fall. During the winter, most of the warm season grasses have a warm beige color. During very hot or dry weather, warm-season grasses will go dormant. This is why they are so successful in surviving the Great Plains' weather. With timely irrigations, they will remain actively growing and retain their color throughout the growing season.

Cool-season grasses grow during the cooler portions of the growing season. They begin to turn green earlier than warm-season grasses and go dormant following the fall's hard freeze. Generally speaking, cool season grasses are more shade-tolerant and will withstand more traffic than warm-season grasses. Most lawns in the Aurora-Denver area have a cool-season grass as their primary turfgrass.

Another differentiation between grasses is whether they are sod-forming or bunch-forming. Sod-forming grasses spread by rhizomes (underground roots) or stolons (above ground roots). Eventually the sod-forming grasses will knit together to form one dense mat. Bunch-forming grasses form in small groups or masses. If most of the bunch-forming grasses are mowed regularly and irrigated during establishment, they will form a dense mat. But if the bunch-formers go into a stress situation due to lack of water or mowing, they tend to retreat back into small clumps.

Alternative Low-Water Requiring Turfgrasses

Table 2-1 lists a number of grasses which may be used for lawns. There is a great variety of texture, density, durability, color, shade tolerance, water, soil and management requirements. Note that the table lists **improved** varieties which should be used in this region. These varieties have been proven to be hardy in our region.

INTRODUCED GRASSES

If a water-conserving lawn with a traditional look is desired, one of the introduced grasses from Table 2-1 should perhaps be selected. Tall fescue varieties, with proper management, will look and feel like a Kentucky bluegrass lawn-while on the average use one-third to one-half less water. "Fairway" crested wheatgrass and smooth brome have leaves that are green and straight, but wider than those of conventional turfgrasses. These varieties will give a lawn different texture. This difference may not be noticeable if such a turf is physically separated from a grass of finer texture by a landscape barrier, such as a planting bed, sidewalk or driveway. Fairway and brome may cut water use on the average by one-half or more without compromising the quality of the turf.

NATIVE GRASSES

Native grasses will appeal to those who enjoy open spaces and meadows that provide a continuous source of interest. Native grasses come in a variety of colors and textures. These characteristics may change with the seasons. If cool-season grasses and warm-season grasses are mixed together and allowed to grow unmowed in a "native meadow", a lawn with a continuous source of interest can be created.

Two native species of turfgrasses are buffalograss and blue grama (Colorado's state grass). They are both short grasses, growing no more than six inches high. Their flowering stems will grow a bit taller. Buffalograss forms a tight sod which resembles a carpet. Its roots may extend to a depth of six feet or more. On the other hand, blue grama is a bunch grass which with a monthly mowing during the summer, will behave as a sod. If blue grama is allowed to grow unmowed, a homeowner will be treated to one of the more captivating of the wild grass flowers.

Buffalograss and blue grama have curly green to gray-green leaves. Both are warm-season grasses, growing and making seed during the warm days of the month. During very hot or dry weather, they will go dormant. This is the reason why they have been so successful in surviving Great Plains weather. With timely irrigations, they will remain actively growing and retain their color throughout the growing seasons.

The other natives listed in Table 2-1 are cool-season grasses. Western, streambank and thickspike wheatgrasses are all sod-forming turf grasses with fairly coarse, straight, blue to blue-green leaves.

ESTABLISHING LAWNS

There are two methods of establishing a lawn, sodding or seeding. The fastest way of establishing a turf grass is by sodding an area. This also minimizes the potential runoff and erosion from the site. Unfortunately, a homeowner's choice of grasses is limited, if he/she decides to use sod. There are typically only a few grasses that are available in sod. To establish sod, follow the nursery's or sod company's instructions.

Seeding allows a homeowner to have more choices in turf grasses. Seeding can also be a lot less expensive than sodding. To find out what seed varieties are available, look at Table 2-1. To meet the needs of the design, a mixture of different grasses may be needed. Go to a reputable seed company and ask for the species and variety that will work for the home's landscape plan. Be sure to know the size of the area that needs to be seeded. A representative from the seed company will be glad to determine how much seed the area needs.

PLANTING SOD OR SEED

Before installing or enlarging a lawn, the City of Aurora requires that a homeowner obtain a lawn permit. The permit requires that the soil be properly prepared (rototilled) with a minimum of three cubic yards of organic matter and 10lbs of treble superphosphate (0-46-0). Organic matter can be compost, peat moss or aged manure. There is a limitation on the amount of high-water requiring turf that may be installed as a lawn. That amount is dependent on the total size of the lot. For more information about the Aurora Lawn Ordinance, contact the Water Conservatin Office at 695-7381.

Planting Grass Seed

After the soil has been properly prepared, broadcast the seed with a rotary spreader, a drop seeder or by hand. Both the spreader and seeder are available at local rental centers. Next, rake the area to get some soil coverage of the seed. Seeds need to be placed at the proper depth (¼"-½") and surrounded by firm, moist soil. Large seeds can be placed deeper than small ones, and seeds should be planted deeper in sandy soils than in clay soils. Lightly irrigate afterwards to firm the seedbed.

With every type of grass, water is necessary for prompt, successful establishment. The seedbed should be maintained in a moist (but not wet) condition until seedlings are well-established and an uniform ground cover is achieved.

With irrigation, cool-season grasses may be planted from spring through mid-summer. They can also be seeded in late August to early September as long as the hot days of summer have passed. Make sure that the seed is planted in time to develop root systems and store food before the first killing frost in the fall. Warm-season grasses will establish best if seeded in May or June.

Seeding Without Irrigation

If irrigation is not possible, planting dates become more critical. Cool-season grasses should not be planted later than April 30. Getting the seeds sown by the end of March is best. Warm-season grasses should be planted during May.

MANAGEMENT DURING THE ESTABLISHMENT PERIOD

Weeding and irrigating are the two major concerns when establishing turf seed beds. Weeding is best accomplished with mowing at a three inch height. Until grasses are fairly well-developed, there is a risk of injury from herbicides, even from those labeled for selective broadleaved weed control.

ORNAMENTAL GRASSES

Another design component includes using grasses as ornamental plants. They may be used as visual buffers, background plantings, borders, specimen plants and in massed plantings.

Tall ornamental grasses are an option. Some tall ornamentals include pampasgrass, plumegrass, maidengrass and fountaingrass. They have graceful, arching foliage and distinctive seed heads. These grasses may be planted alone and used as specimen plants, or used as a contrasting background for other plants. They have attractive seed heads which may be used in indoor flower arrangements. Blue fescue lends itself to attractive borders and massed plantings. Most of these tall ornamental grasses are available from local nurseries as potted plants.

Tall native grasses may also be used as ornamentals, but they are only available in seed. Native tall grasses such as big bluestem, prairie sandreed, yellow indiangrass, switchgrass and reed canarygrass may be used to embellish the landscapes with distinctive colors and textures. Big bluestem turns a red-orange in the fall which persists through much of the winter. Prairie sandreed can grow up to seven feet tall and has seed heads reminiscent of pampasgrass. But native tall grasses have definite soil needs. Prairie sandreed needs sandy soil, while reed canarygrass needs a moist site. Big bluestem, switchgrass and indiangrass prefer well-drained soils which receive extra moisture.

Shorter native grasses can also be used as ornamental grasses. These grasses such as little bluestem, sideoats grama, indian ricegrass and blue grama, will grow nearly anywhere except in the shade and wet areas. Little bluestem and sideoats grama exhibit strong red-orange fall color and have very distinctive seed

heads. With the exception of blue grama, these grasses will grow from 18″ to 30″ tall. They may be used for borders or in massed plantings and rock gardens in association with other plants. Combining appropriate native grasses with wildflowers can turn a simple "landscape" into a dynamic one! See Table 2-2 for a listing of ornamental grasses that can be used in a residential landscape.

MAINTAINING AN ESTABLISHED LAWN

Once the grass has been established, the real challenge emerges with keeping water consumption down. Unfortunately at this time, very little research has been done on the fertilizer needs, disease and insect problems on low-water requiring grasses. But much time and research has been given to the fertilization needs, disease and insect problems of Kentucky bluegrass. This area is addressed in Chapter 7. Tips on how to carefully irrigate a turf area are given in Chapter 3 on "Proper Irrigation".

keep lawn 2 inches or more for deeper roots

TABLE 2-1
Water Conserving Grasses for Residential Lawns

Species	Variety 1	Characteristics 2	Sandy	Loamy	Clayey	Seed Rate lbs. PLS per 1000 sq. ft.	
Tall Fescue Festuca arundinacea	Apolo, Falcon Mustang, Olympia	I,C,B		x	x	5.0	Naturally a bunchgrass, but forms a sod when regularly mowed; turf type varieties resemble Kentucky bluegrass; many new turf-type varieties are now available; will tolerate sandy soil if watered regularly.
Crested Wheatgrass Agropyron cristatum	Fairway	I,C,B	x	x	x	5.0	A bunchgrass which will form a sod if seeded heavily and mowed occasionally.
Smooth brome Bromus inermis	Lincoln Manchar	I,C,S,	x	x	x	5.0	A taller, coarser-leaved green pasture and hay grass; needs more frequent mowing than all of the other grasses except for tall fescue.
Buffalograss Bouchloe dactyloides	Sharp's Improved, or Texoka	N,W,S		x	x	bur 3.0 grain 1.0	A native, low growing sod-former; tolerates periodic mowing at a 3" height; separate male and female plants buy treated seed to assure good germination; spread by stolons.
Blue grama Bouteloua gracillis	Lovington	N,W,B	x	x	x	1.0	A native bunch grass which will form a "mat" if seeded heavily and mowed occasionally at a 3" height; appearance similar to buffalograss.
Blue grama- Buffalograss (50-50 mix)	See above	-	x	x	x	½ ea of above rates	A less expensive alternative to pure buffalograss seeding
Western Wheatgrass Agropyron smithii	Arriba	N,C,S		x	x	5.0	A native grass with leaf colors ranging from blue and blue-gray to green; tolerates periodic mowing at a 3" height.
Streambank Wheatgrass Agropyron riparium	Sodar	N,C,S	x	x	x	5.0	A smaller, finer-leaved grass than western or thickspike; "streambank" is a misnomer-it doesn't like moist sites.
Thickspike Wheatgrass Agropyron dasystachyum	Critana	N,C,S	x	x		5.0	Similar to western wheatgrass but prefers and (out-performs western on) sandier sites

1. Although these grasses can endure periods of drought and heat, they all require irrigation for establishment. Once established, irrigation is necessary only during extended dry spells or to help retain attractive color.

2. CHARACTERISTICS:
   N=Native; I=Introduced (not native to the Front Range); C=Cool Season; W=Warm Season; B=Bunchgrass; S=Sod former

TABLE 2-2
Ornamental Grasses for Landscape Accents

Species	Variety	Characteristics 2	Sandy	Loamy	Clayey	Mature Height	
Prairie sandreed Calamovilfa longifolia	Goshen	N,W,S	x	x		60"	Tall, attractive flower; plants turn pale gold at maturity; will spread; adapted to Plains and lower Foothills.
Big bluestem Andropogon gerardii	Kaw	N,W,S	x	x		60"	Plants turn reddish-purple color at maturity and red-orange in the fall; unusual "fuzzy" seeds adapted to Foothills and Plains.
Sand bluestem Andropogon hallii	Elida	N,W,S	x	x	x	60"	Same as above but generally restricted to Plains.
Switchgrass Panicum virgatum	Nebraska 28	N,W,S	x	x	x	36"	Becomes reddish-orange at maturity; prefers sites with extra moisture in the Plains.
Indiangrass Sorghastrum nutans	Holt	N,W,S	x			60"	Color changes to bronze at maturity; prefers moist sandy sites in the Plains and rocky sites in the lower Foothills; can reach 8ft. in height in moist sandy areas.
Little bluestem Schizachyrium scoparium	Pastura	N,W,B	x	x	x	24"	Resembles big and sand bluestem, but is smaller; Plains, Foothills and Mountains; red-orange fall color; attractive "fuzzy" seeds.
Sideoats grama Bouteloua curtipendula	Vaughn	N,W,B	x	x	x	15"	Plant turns reddish-orange at maturity; seeds dangle from one side of stem resembling an indian's war lance; adapted to Plains, Foothills and Mountains.
Indian ricegrass Oryzopsis hymenoides	Paloma	N,C,B	x	x	x	18"	Interesting, "delicate-appearing" plant with seeds resembling tiny pearls; low germination rates because of "hard" seed; helps to plant in fall; adapted to Plains, Mountains and Foothills.
Reed canarygrass Phalaris arundinacea	Loreed	N,C,S		x	x	60"	Robust, aggressive grass in wetter sites; attractive seed heads; can become a nuisance in some situations; adapted to Plains, Foothills and Mountains.
Arizona fescue Festuca arizonica	Redondo	N,C,B	x	x		18"	An attractive bunchgrass of the Mountains; needs some supplemental moisutre to be grown at lower elevations; found naturally in Mountains and Foothills.

1. No seeding rates are given since the amounts are so small. Seeding rates for large areas are available at the local U.S. Soil Conservation Service office.

2. See Footnote #2 in Table 2-1

Proper Irrigation

Proper irrigation has perhaps the greatest potential to affect water savings than any other component of a water-conserving landscape. Improper irrigation methods, system leaks and poor irrigation practices can waste many gallons of water. Whether the landscape has an automatic or portable irrigation system, the watering method should evenly distribute water throughout the entire landscape.

Irrigation industry professionals claim that a properly designed and properly operated irrigation system can reduce a minimum of 20% of water each year. Experts also claim that 85% of all landscape problems in the metro area are directly related to over-watering. Here are some things to think about when choosing an irrigation system.

CRITERIA FOR CHOOSING AN IRRIGATION SYSTEM

Before choosing an irrigation system, it is important to understand three basic facts:

— Different plants have different water requirements.

— Specific types of plants will have varying water needs depending on size, age and location in the landscape.

— Individual plant or lawn areas have water requirements which vary constantly with season, weather, age and previous watering methods.

Remember, the landscape design should group plants with similar water needs together in order for optimal irrigation and water savings. The design should also address the irrigation head's optimal water throwing distance and differentiate between turf and planting beds in order to avoid overspray.

AUTOMATIC VERSUS PORTABLE

Automatic irrigation systems require less manual labor and time from a homeowner than a portable system. Automatic systems also have a timer or controller that automatically shuts off the water after a set period of time. Yet, automatic irrigation systems are more expensive and require excavation in order to install.

Portable systems on the other hand, are less expensive and allow the homeowner more flexibility in changing the landscape without having to redesign the irrigation system. But portable systems do require the homeowner to manually turn on faucets and move hoses throughout the landscape.

Even Water Distribution Pattern

All automatic or portable systems should evenly distribute water throughout the entire landscape. To determine how much water and how evenly an existing system is distributing water, set out four flat-bottomed, short cans (such as tuna or cat food cans). Place each can at various distances from the irrigation heads. Turn the system on for a half hour. Then turn off the system and measure the amount of water in each can. This will give a homeowner a good idea of the system's water distribution pattern.

To determine how much water the system distributes in one half hour, take the measurements of the four cans and add them together. Divide that total by four to get the average amount of water that the system delivers in a half hour period of time. Then multiply that total by two in order to get the amount of water the system delivers in a hour's time.

Flexibility In Reaching Different Irrigation Zones

Again, plants have different water needs. The irrigation system should also be designed to provide different amounts of water to be placed on different landscape areas. This is why it is so vital for the landscape design to include zoned irrigation. Plants that have similar water needs should be placed together. To meet those needs, the automatic sprinkler system or portable sprinkler should only distribute enough water to each area to meet the plants' needs.

Irrigation equipment should include heads that deliver a pattern of water close to the ground. This allows the water to be less prone to wind deflection and evaporation.

Determination Of Pressure

Another important aspect in choosing an irrigation system is determining the area's water pressure. Since water pressure varies throughout the metro area, anyone planning a irrigation system should call their local utilities or water department for the water pressure reading in their area or have the pressure tested on site for greater accuracy.

CHOOSING AN AUTOMATIC IRRIGATION SYSTEM

Points to Consider When Choosing an Automatic Irrigation System

When choosing an automatic irrigation system, consider these points:

1. Decide what type of system (sprayhead or rotary) will work best with the house's landscaped area.

2. Determine which system will best cover the size and shape of the area to be watered. Covering the area with the least amount of heads is an economic factor.

3. Realize that areas of turf, shrubs and flowers will require different irrigation heads and different amounts of water.

31

4. What is the house's water pressure? Low water pressure means a lower flow of water and low-pressure type irrigation heads. Low water pressure increases the required number of irrigation heads.

5. Once installed, consider the environment of the area-the wind, rain and temperature.

6. Once installed, determine the soil's ability to accept water.

There are many local irrigation centers, contractors and specialists who can assist residents in choosing and designing the appropriate automatic irrigation system that will meet the landscape's needs.

BASIC TYPES OF IRRIGATION SYSTEMS

There are two basic types of automatic irrigation systems (in various forms) that are available on the landscape market. They are:

— pop-up sprayhead
— pop-up rotary heads

Sprayhead System

The most widely used is the sprayhead irrigation system. There are many varieties of sprayhead irrigation systems, including heads which do not pop up; pop-up types which will extend above the grass from one to six inches; shrub spray heads which have a fixed pattern used in shrub beds, and the bubbler types used to flood flower beds. The 4″ pop-up sprayheads are best for smaller or more intricately shaped lawn areas.

The main features of sprayhead irrigation heads are:

1. The heads emit fine sheets or fans of water.

2. The heads operate at low pressures of 20 to 30 pounds per square inch (psi).

3. The heads cover a radius of 5 to 15 feet.

4. The system applies one to two inches of water per hour.

Rotary Irrigation System

The second type of automatic irrigation systems is the rotary head systems. These water-driven units are recommended for large open residential lawns or multi-family complexes. The main features of the rotary drive head irrigation systems are:

1. Single or double nozzles with water streams revolving over the area.

2. Interchangeable nozzles for various precipitation rates and psi applications.

3. Operate on 30 to 60 psi and higher gallons of water per minute.

4. The heads cover a radius of 25 to 60 feet.

5. Apply water at rates of ⅛ to ½ inch per hour.

6. Most economical for large, open turf areas.

7. Wind does not affect rotary irrigation systems as much as sprayhead systems.

Controllers

A component that should be used with automatic sprinklers is a controller or timer. A controller is simply a clock that opens and closes electrically-operated valves for preset time periods. Recent advances in controller technology and design provide greater flexibility in watering schedules. One option available in several controllers is the ability to have different watering schedules for turf and garden areas.

There are also automatic timing devices for portable systems. These range from sophisticated multifunction systems to simple mechanical spring valves. These devices can be extremely useful, but care should be taken to select a durable, reliable timer.

Because the controller is the only portion of the irrigation system that is frequently adjusted and is the most important element in determining the length of water application, it should be carefully selected to suit specific needs.

PORTABLE IRRIGATION SYSTEMS

There are many types of portable irrigation systems. Some of the most common types of portable systems are:

— Stationary fan system

— Oscillating-arm system

— Whirling-head system

— Pulsating system

— Plastic sprinkler bases

Again, the main criteria for choosing any type of irrigation system is to be sure that the water distribution pattern is even. Even portable irrigation systems of the same type have completely different patterns. Without knowing this, a homeowner can end up with over and under watered sections of lawn.

sprinklers with coarse, low spray are best

DRIP IRRIGATION

The concept behind drip irrigation is to provide the plant with the optimal soil moisture environment. This is accomplished by directing water directly to individual plants via small tubing or emitters. Drip irrigation saves water because only the plant's root zone is supplied with water, and very little water is lost to evaporation and percolation if the proper amount of water is applied.

Drip irrigation systems work best for shrubs and trees. Turf and some groundcover areas are more economically and evenly watered by overhead sprinklers. A combination of overhead sprinklers for turf areas and drip for shrubbery and trees may provide the ideal system for a homeowner.

Drip irrigation systems are not only ideal for level land, but are also useful for slopes. They can be a real aid in erosion control since there is very little surface runoff. The installation of a properly designed drip irrigation system is much less than the cost of other systems, while maintenance is minimal.

Drip irrigation can also be automated. It may be included with an automatic irrigation system and controlled by the system's timer.

OTHER IRRIGATION METHODS

Soil soakers are a cheaper but not quite as efficient substitute for drip irrigation. Soil soakers are long tubes of plastic or canvas with rows of tiny holes. Like drip irrigation tubes, they can be placed wherever necessary over trees' and shrubs' root systems. With the holes facing down, the soaker can be connected to a garden hose and left in place indefinitely.

Another alternative to a drip irrigation system is described below. Place a perforated coffee can or plastic jug with a lid over the root system of a tree or shrub on the soil's surface and fill it with water. The water will slowly drip through the holes and into the ground.

A deep-root irrigator is a great method to water trees and shrubs. This device is a large needle attached to the end of a hose. The needle is inserted into the ground over the root system. When its valve is opened, it can emit water 12 to 18 inches deep into the soil. It can also be used to fertilize roots. Depending on the type of trees and shrubs being watered, a schedule of deep-watering trees and shrubs once a month should be adequate. This method should not be used on newly planted material during its first year.

Use of Runoff Water

For sloped areas, runoff water will always be a problem. Here are some ideas on how to capture runoff water and use it beneficially.

1. Individual earth or decorative basins around trees and shrubs will hold water until it seeps into the ground.

2. Shallow irrigation ditches next to rows of plants will serve the same purpose.

3. If plants have been installed during the hot dry summer months, special care should be given to protect them from heat stress. Heat stress occurs when a plant releases or transpires more water than it can take up from its small root system. This is more likely during hot windy weather. Since the root system is only so large, adding too much water to the soil will not help the plant and may actually harm it. The best way to relieve heat stress in a plant is to spray its foliage with a fine mist of water. This causes the plant to stop transpiring water. In most plants, the leaves will fully recover in about an hour. Even while not showing signs of stress, pines and spruces will almost always benefit from a light spraying. Some experts feel that spraying of roses, junipers and other evergreen shrubs with broad leaves should be avoided. Water can remain on the leaves and during the heat of the day, the water may actually boil and damage the leaves.

Winter Watering

An important part of an irrigation schedule is winter watering. The metro area usually experiences some long periods of dry, sunny days during the winter. Thus, the plants like trees and shrubs are not able to get the water that they need in order to survive. Deciduous plants need some soil moisture in the winter to prevent damage to the root system. Evergreen plants require water because they are still using water daily. Even a turf area will benefit from monthly winter water. Lack of water - not extreme cold, is the biggest cause of "winter kill" in all plants.

A landscape will require water if snowfall or late rains have not fallen during the month. A persisting blanket of snow will stop evaporation and delay the need for additional water. A recommended amount of water added is ¾ inch of water to lawn and plants at least once a month.

Winter watering should be done on days when no snow cover is present, the air temperature is above freezing, and early enough in the day to allow the water to percolate into the soil before freezing night temperatures. Frozen, dry soil will absorb water slowly as long as the water does not freeze on the surface.

Be sure to winter water by hand. All automatic irrigation systems should be drained prior to the first hard frost. Any water remaining in the system's pipe would freeze and might cause damage to the pipes.

WHEN TO WATER

Perhaps the most important step in irrigation is knowing when to water. **The average turf areas in the denver metro area need up to 1″ of precipitation and/or irrigation water per week in the spring and fall, and up to 1½″ of precipitation and/or irrigation water per week in the summer.**

The best watering schedule for clay soils in the Denver metro area is to water every third day. Water sandy soils every day. The best time to water clay or sandy soils is in the early morning. This then reduces the amount of water lost to evaporation or wind.

Other watering tips are:

1. Use your irrigation system's clock. The new programmable clocks can be a great convenience to a homeowner, but people tend to set them and forget them. This does not enable the system to be flexible or responsive to changing conditions which affect the landscape's need for water. Adjust the system's water schedule for seasonal requirements and turn off the system in order to take advantage of rainfalls.

2. Watch the E/T rate published in the local newspapers and shown on the three major television networks' local news shows. The E/T rate is the amount of moisture lost by (Kentucky bluegrass) turf in the previous three days. Then by following the E/T three-day schedule and making allowances for rainfalls during the three-day period, water the amount of water given for that day's E/T rate.

Watering Trees, Shrubs and Perrenials

Different plants have different watering needs. The best way to determine a plant's water needs is to:

1. Look at its appearance. Leaves and needles should be a normal color and texture. Any dryness, brittleness or drooping of leaves or needles indicates the immediate need for water. Yellowing or loss of still soft leaves or needles indicates that the plant may be drowning in too much water.

2. Test the soil. Dig down with a hand trowel and feel the soil at the depth of 3-6 inches. If you can easily dig and make a ball with the soil in your hand, then it has a good water content. Very hard soil would indicate the need for water, while a muddy soil would indicate that too much water has been applied.

SUMMARY

Proper irrigation is a very important factor in Xeriscape. Over 50% of the water that is used in the metro area is used to water landscaped areas. By zoning plants with similar needs, designing a system to meet only the water needs and using simple watering tips, a homeowner can often significantly reduce the amount of water that he/she uses.

deep water trees and shrubs

Soils and Soil Improvement

The Denver metro area's dry climate does not provide our soils with a great deal of decomposed organic matter or humus in the soil. It is not only **necessary** to add organic matter and other amendments to improve the condition of the soil, but soil preparation is also an important water conservation measure.

COMPOSITION OF SOIL

The average "composition" of soil (by weight) is:

45% Minerals
(clay, silt, sand, gravel and stones)

25% Water
(the amount will vary with precipitation and soil texture)

25% Air
(an essential ingredient for roots and living organisms within the soil)

5% Organic Matter
(both living and dead organisms)

There are many other characteristics that make soils different from one or another, such as texture, structure, permeability, depth, erosion potential and fertility.

Soil Texture

A soil is composed primarily of particles of sand, silt or clay. It is these particles that give soil its texture. Texture is the relative proportion of sand, silt and clay particles in soil.

Sand particles range in size from 2 millimeters (mm.) to .05 mm in diameter. One millimeter is about the thickness of a dime. Sand particles are easily seen and feel gritty. Silt particles are between .05 mm. and .0002 mm. in diameter and have the feel of flour. Clay particles are less than .0002 mm. in diameter and feel sticky when wet.

Soil Fertility

Each type of plant has different soil fertility needs. The Colorado State University Cooperative Extension can run tests from samples of soil from a homeowner's garden, flower bed and lawn areas. Call the local county Colorado State University Cooperative Extension for instructions for taking and mailing the samples. There will be a small charge for the test. The tests' report will include recommendations of fertilization needs, depending on the plant material that will be grown in that area. The report will assess the major and secondary nutrients needed for the health and vigor for specific type of plants (i.e. wood, perennial or turf) in that area.

Soil Around New Residences

When most homes are built, the soil around them is usually altered. The original top layer may be removed in the grading of the lot, or it may have been covered by material from previous excavations. In spots, it may be filled with rocks and debris left by the builders. The regions against the foundation of the house are especially likely to be filled with poor soil and debris. Whether the soil has been untouched or altered, it may be far from ideal for growing turf, perennials and other plants. The soil should be amended to suit the individual needs of the plants that are to be planted within its areas.

The solutions to improving clay, sandy or poor soil left by the builder are the same: amend the soil by rototilling organic matter and phosphate into the soil. Benefits to amending the soil are:

a) Loosens a clayey soil

b) Allows air and water to circulate within the soil

c) Allows the organic matter to act as a sponge in sandy soil

d) Serves as a "bank" for storing nutrients

e) Increase the organic content of the soil

Soils in the Metro Area

Most soils in the metro area have too much clay or too much sand. Water quickly soaks into a sandy soil, but sandy soil can hold very little of it. This then requires homeowners to water the landscape on a more frequent basis. In clay soils, water is not easily absorbed and runs off. But clay soils can hold much more water than sandy soils. Water will not move through the clay soils easily because it is held tightly by the clay particles. These two soil types create situations where plant life can dry out and wilt (sandy soils) or "drown" due to an excess of water (clay soils).

CITY OF AURORA'S LAWN PERMIT ORDINANCE

The City of Aurora requires, and experts recommend, that if installing or enlarging a turf area, residents must use a minimum of three cubic yards of organic matter and 10 lbs of treble super phosphate (0-46-0) per thousand square feet of turf area. Organic matter can be compost, peat moss or aged manure. This material needs to be rototilled or disced into the soil at a minimum depth of six inches. There is also a limitation on the amount of (Kentucky bluegrass) turf that a citizen may install in their lawn. For more information about the Aurora Lawn Permit Ordinance, contact the Aurora Utilities Department's Water Conservation Office.

ORGANIC MATTER

According to Colorado State University Cooperative Extension, the best organic amendments for soil include relatively coarse, partially decomposed compost, and aged barnyard manure. The type of manure is not important, but it should be aged at least one year. Fresh manure can be odorous and too high in ammonia, which injures plant roots. Because of high salts, repeated use of feedlot manure should be avoided, unless the salts are first leached. Dairy cattle manure generally is lower in salt content. Many experts discourage the use of "mountain peat moss" due to its low organic content and because its mining threatens mountain meadow ecosystems.

add organic matter. it improves the water efficiency of the soil

LIQUID AMENDMENTS

Several liquid products are now on the market. Their promoters claim that these liquid "amendments" will "break up or condition the soil." Most actually act as wetting agents. They break the surface tension of water around the soil particles thus allowing deeper water penetration. They don't increase the pore space of a soil. At best, they may provide a temporary improvement of water penetration, but they don't actually alter the soil.

POLYACRYLAMIDES OR POLYMERS

A new landscape innovation is the use of polymers or polyacrylamides. In their original state, they look like small beads or powder. They often have the ability to absorb 40 times their weight in water. When mixed with soil, they improve a soil's ability to store water for plant growth. They also may help to keep a soil loose from expansion and contraction as water is absorbed and released. **This may not however, be desirable near a foundation, sidewalk or driveway.**

Many agencies, park districts, and landscapers have found that selected use of polymers can help reduce water consumption, protect new plants during their first years of establishment, and reduce some water runoff. Polymers are well-suited to use in landscaping areas which will not receive regular watering and aid in the establishment of newly planted wood species.

PURE HUMIC ACID (LEONARDITE)

A new landscape material that has just appeared in the residential landscaping market is humic acid. Humic acid is a material from stripping of coal mines. It is taken into the soil by precipitation. Supporters claim that humic acids help improve soil structure, soil chemistry, and plants. It has been used in reclamation projects in high altitude climates.

Erosion Control

A key problem in many areas along the Front Range, is erosion control.

Mulches

Cover the planting beds with an optimum level of three inches of mulch. A 3"-4" level will discourage weeds. Yet a depth deeper than 5", depending on the type of mulch and growing conditions, will discourage plant growth and encourage the plants to root in the mulch rather than the soil. Mulches are covered in depth in Chapter 5.

Live Mulch

Use of a spreading groundcover is another option in controlling erosion. Until the groundcover completely covers the area, use a mulch to cover the bare soil. A list of groundcovers is given in Chapter 6.

Contouring

Straight lines of a rectangular flower bed do not fit well with curving slopes. Plant beds whose lines follow the natural contour of the slope. This allows the bed to be both practical and pleasing to the eye. Rows that follow horizontally across the slope rather than vertical lines, also help control runoff and reduce erosion.

Terracing

If a slope is steep, there will be a great deal of water runoff. To avoid this, terraces are needed at intervals to intercept the runoff. Terraces are like little dams through a flower bed or hillside allowing each ridge to have runoff from the top tiers.

With small garden plots, miniature terraces can be used by following the contour lines at intervals of 15 to 30 feet. A two to three foot wide channel with a depth of one foot is usually sufficient. Be sure to reinforce the ridge with heavy piles of fill across gullies or depressions. It may take some trial and error to find the size that will withstand the normal runoff for the plot.

Several ordinances in Aurora address the specific issue of erosion control. Any area with bare soil has the potential for an erosion problem. In the surburban areas, bare soil areas are usually found in planting beds, new turf areas or slopes. There are several avenues to tackle this problem. For more information about the city's erosion control ordinances, contact the Aurora Community Services Department.

MORE INFORMATION ABOUT SOILS

Your local county Colorado State University Cooperative Extension has information sheets on soils for garden areas, vegetable areas, trees and other plants. They will also run a soil sample test for a small fee. The report will include recommendations of fertilizers to suite the conditions shown by the test. Soil tests may also be obtained from private soil testing labs.

Another source of information is the U.S. Department of Agriculture's Soil Conservation Service. They will provide onsite assistance and help with erosion control. The SCS has prepared soil surveys, which include soil maps, soil descriptions and soil interpretations. From these soil surveys, they can answer such questions as 1) what kinds of plants can be grown; 2) what will it take to grow them; 3)what will the yield and quality be, and 4) what will happen to the soil in the process. The local offices of the Soil Conservation Service are listed in the U.S. Government blue pages, under the U.S. Department of Agriculture.

Use of Mulches

A mulch can be defined as any organic or inorganic material used to protect the soil from moisture loss and/or improve the soil condition when applied to the soil's surface.

Since mulches do not compete with plants for water, they act as an ideal low-water requiring replacement for turf areas. Mulches also reduce the amount of water evaporated from the soil's surface by lowering the surface temperature. Mulches may also:

— help plants more effectively use water that falls naturally as rain or from irrigation.

— reduce the soil's temperature by acting as a cover,

— improve water penetration and air movement in the soil by reducing soil surface crusting,

— control in many cases, soil temperature fluctuations,

— reduce soil erosion,

— protect shallow-rooted plants from freeze damage and frost-heave,

— delay emergence of early spring bulbs to avoid damage due to early spring freezing,

— improve the soil's fertility,

— may slightly increase soil acidity,

— reduce soil compaction,

— create more visual appeal around plant beds, and

— visually separate different landscape zones

An ideal mulch should not compact too easily. A tightly compacted mulch can obstruct water and air from leaving or entering the soil and the plants' roots. The compacted mulch may also create a layer in which plants (such as weeds) begin to root. A mulch should also not pose a fire hazard to the area.

Inorganic and Organic Mulches

There are two basic types of mulches-inorganic and organic. Organic mulches will decompose and improve the soil, while inorganic mulches do not decompose as quickly and tend to portray a more formal effect. Organic mulches include wood and bark chips, straw and grass clippings. Inorganic mulches include gravel, boulders and lava rock.

Homeowners should be aware of the possibility of nitrogen deficiency with the decomposing of organic mulch. As organic mulches decompose, some of the soil's nitrogen is used by the breakdown organisms. Consequently, nitrogen deficiency may occur. A sign of nitrogen deficiency is a yellowing of plant material, primarily of the lower leaves. When this occurs, nitrogen fertilizers should be added to the surrounding plant materials. Consult the local county Colorado State University Extension for more information on what type of fertilizer to use.

Factors to Consider When Choosing Mulches

What type of mulch should a homeowner use? Again, each homeowner has different needs and themes with their landscapes. Consider these factors when choosing a mulch:

— If the primary reason for using a mulch is to improve the soil, use an organic mulch. According to the Colorado State University Cooperative Extension, an organic mulch which gradually breaks down over time should be the first choice.

— If the theme of the landscape plan is to convey a formal effect, then consider using an inorganic mulch such as rock or gravel which decompose very slowly.

— Another factor influencing the type of mulch to be used, is the type of plant material to be mulched. If the area is used primarily as a flower bed, use an organic mulch which can be easily turned under with the soil each fall.

— Cost is probably the largest factor when choosing a mulch. Many inorganic mulches, such as rock and gravel, can be expensive and diffcult to transport. Organic mulches tend to be less expensive and easier to transport and spread.

When to Apply Mulches

If the mulch is used to control weeds or for aesthetics, it should be spread before the weeds begin to come up. Otherwise the weeds will have a toehold on the area. If the mulches are intended primarily to protect new transplants from freezes in the fall, mulches should be applied soon after transplanting. If the mulch is to be used to reduce frost-heave and delay spring growth with such plants as crocus and other bulbs, the mulch should be applied after the ground has been frozen.

Homeowners generally have two choices when applying mulches. He/she can apply a 3"-4" depth of mulch on the top of the soil's surface or apply a layer of mulch over a geotextile fabric. A geotextile fabric is a woven fabric that acts as a weed barrier. BLACK PLASTIC SHOULD NOT BE USED AS A WEED BARRIER. The trouble with black plastic is that it does not allow the water and air to enter or leave the soil. This then does not allow the roots of trees and shrubs that are underneath the black plastic to get the water that they need. This in turn, may stress the tree or shrub.

Without the use of geotextile fabrics, most mulches should be applied to a depth of three to four inches. According to Colorado State Unviersity Cooperative Extension, straw, dried leaves and similar materials need to be applied to a depth of at least six inches. Some of these mulches, particularly straw and loose leaves, may harbor rodents. When using such mulches, don't place them closer than six inches to the base of woody plants. When these mulches are placed next to the plants, rodents living in the mulch can chew the bark of the plants and may kill the plants. (See Table 5-1 on organic and inorganic mulches.)

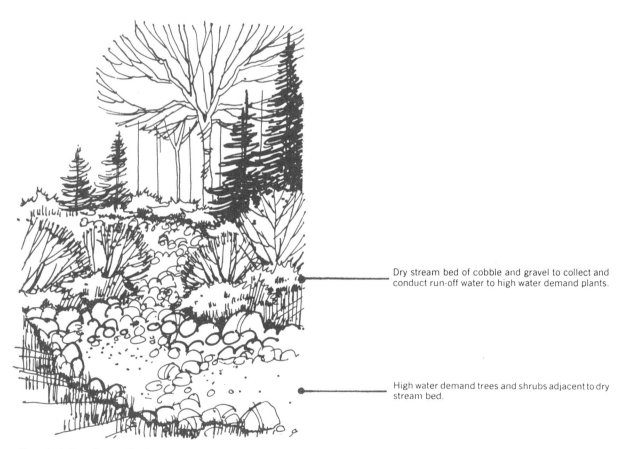

Dry stream bed of cobble and gravel to collect and conduct run-off water to high water demand plants.

High water demand trees and shrubs adjacent to dry stream bed.

Sketch 4. Dry Steam Bed

TABLE 5-1

This table gives you an overview of the benefits and challenges of different mulches commonly used in Colorado

ORGANIC

Name	Benefits	Challenges
Shredded Wood/ Shredded Tree Trimmings	Doesn't compact, so it allows free movement of air and water. Does not easily blow away in the wind. Clings easily to steep slopes.	Weathers to a grey color. Coarse in appearance.
Wood Chips	Neater in apearance than shredded wood. Long-lasting and attractive.	Does not cling well on steep slopes. Variable in texture and color, sometimes not uniform in appearance.
Bark	Same benefits as wood chips. Comes in several sizes- fine, medium and large. Much user appeal and expensive. More bark needed if large and coarse to adequately cover over soil surface and prevent weed growth. May be used for informal walkways.	Same challenges as wood chips. Cost relatively high.
Residues - (straw, hay, leaves, compost and lawn clippings)	Decompose rapidly and improves soil. Best for intensively worked areas, i.e. vegetable and flower gardens. Best and easiest application for straw and hay is to lay it in "books" or sections as it breaks off the bale. Stays in place well. Best to shred them before using as mulch.	Hay and straw not very neat looking. Whole, unshredded leaves mat down and repel water and blow easily.
Peat	Commonly used as mulch, but may be used as an amendment.	It blows easily and is expensive. It may introduce weed seeds. It is difficult to "wet" after it has dried. It repels water.
Crushed corncobs	Uniform in color. Variety of colors are available.	May retain too much moisture at surface. May compact if kept wet.
Pine needles	Attractive. Do not compact.	Difficult to obtain in quantity. Somewhat of a fire hazard.
Sawdust	Attractive. Usually available.	Fine sawdust may crust. Some sources, such as walnut, produce toxic substances. Additions of nitrogen are usually necessary.

INORGANIC

Name	Benefits	Challenges
Clay aggregates	Attractive gray and brown colors available.	Relatively expensive.
Rock	Available in many colors. Available in a variety of prices. Very permanent mulch. Will not easily blow away. Cobble mulch can be used to create a rich, bold textural relief. It can also be used to create "dry stream" beds.	Will not prevent growth of some weedy grasses. Should be softened with plants, if used. Wind-born dirt fills crevices between aggregates, creating rooting medium for weeds.
Lava	Has good insulating qualities. Available in rust and grey colors.	Very lightweight. Blows away easily. Does not cling well to slopes. More ornamental than practical.

Use of Low-Water Requiring Plants

There is a wide variety of beautiful, low-water requiring plants that are suitable to the Denver metro area. Homeowners have the choice of many different colors, textures and shapes. Yet, the actual selection of plants for a Xeriscape or any landscape design should not be taken lightly. The investment and longevity of plant material necessitates careful planning and research.

Plants should be chosen with the needs of the homeowner and the landscape design, the local climate, soil and precipitation levels in mind. A homeowner should also consider the plant's drought-tolerance and hardiness to the Denver metro area's weather. The bottom line is that the plants in a landscape should be attractive, low-water requiring and survive the climatical conditions of the area. When choosing plants, consider these suggestions:

1. Find out what the mature height and spread of the plant will be and plan for that height and spread in the design. With trees, the tree's height, spread and shape are called its growth habit. A tree that has a broad shape will tend to be about one-half breadth to its height. Columnar-shaped trees will generally be one-third to one-half in width to the height. Narrow, upright trees will generally have a spread of one-third or less of the height. Nurserymen can generally help describe the growth habit of a tree or any other plant.

2. Consider the plants' shape or form. The basic plant forms are columnar, round, vase, weeping, oval, conical or pyramidal. Limit selection to several different plant types that will serve as the dominant forms in the design.

3. Consider if the plant will attract wildlife. Certain plants' fruits are attractive to birds, while other plants' blooms draw butterflies or bees.

4. Check the local city codes. The Aurora City Code prohibits any trees or thorny or spiky plant material to be planted in a utility easement. They prohibit any thorny or spiky plant material on any public right-of-way.

5. Talk to a nurseryman about the care needed for each plant in the design. Ask about fertilization and watering needs. Find out if the plant is "messy" with dropping seed pods or berries, or if it produces sap.

6. Group plants with similar water needs together. This will help reduce maintenance time and effort.

7. With most plants, the soil must be improved in order to provide a good medium for the plant to establish and get needed moisture. For instance, a clay soil will hold water more tightly than a loamy soil. Due to its greater adhesiveness, the clay soil holds the water with more tension and will not let the water be used by the plant. Adding water more frequently to clay soil does not get additional water to the plant because the water tends to fill up the pore space and may cause oxygen starvation to the plants' roots. On the other extreme, sandy soils will not hold the water long enough for the plants' roots to get access to the water.

Again, the solution to both of these problems is proper soil preparation. Contact your local nurseryman or the local county's Colorado State University Cooperative Extension for information about the soil and moisture needs of specific plants.

8. Know how to properly plant and care for the plants. Improper planting procedures are a frequent cause of plant failure after transplanting. Many nurseries have planting instructions available for customers. Also contact the local county's Colorado State University Coopertive Extension for their service-in-action packets on planting instructions.

PLANTING ALTERNATIVES

When planning a Xeriscape, there are many design options using a variety of plants. One option is the use of groundcovers or some substitute cover like mulch, hard surfaces or gravel. The principle reason for a groundcover is to prevent soil erosion. Yet, groundcovers and substitute covers can define a space, change a landscape's texture or give a "carpet" affect. Areas that must carry concentrated runoff should be permanently paved or protected. Areas that receive a lot of traffic should be covered with a traffic-hardy groundocver, such as turf.

The ideal ground cover plant should have an attractive appearance throughout all four seasons, while giving a year-round cover to the soil. For rapid coverage of an area, the ground cover should have the ability to spread by itself. Species that reproduce with rhizomes or stolons (like the "runners" in strawberries) will cover quickly. In order to create a weed barrier, the groundcover should branch heavily or produce dense foliage close to the ground.

Literally hundreds of plants, including grasses, are suitable as groundcovers in a Xeriscape. They range from creeping plants no more than a few inches high (sedum, hardy ice plant, wolly thyme, creeping juniper) to vigorous shrubs that spread with a dense coverage (forsythia and cotoneaster). Most areas that have living groundcovers require hand weeding once or twice a year as the plants become established. As the season progresses, weeds will come up. Weeding shouldn't be necessary for most landscapes once a healthy mat of groundcover has become established. When trying to establish a groundcover, it's always a good idea to use mulches as an interim cover. Mulches can then act as a barrier, protect the soil from erosion and help reduce the soil temperature.

The next option to consider is planting beds. Herbs, perennials and wildflowers in beds are useful and attractive in a residential Xeriscape. Suggested annual bedding plants for a Xeriscape are: moss rose, marigold, zinnia and sunflower. Some perennials include: alyssum, silver mound sage, lupine, hardy ice plant, sunrose, penstemon, gaillardia, paper flower, prairie coneflower, gay feather, spiderwort and evening primrose. Spring-blubs must have moist soil in the fall, winter and spring, in order to bloom. An idea for arranging wildflowers in a more formal setting is to place the wildflowers in 2¼" pots in masses.

Herbs can be incorporated into rock gardens, or along walls, borders or paths. Among the best for drier sites are lavender, thyme, anise, dill, chives, onions, garlic and sage.

Another option that a homeowner has is mass plantings. Plants such as shrubs and vines can effectively hold and cover slopes with mass plantings. Some small trees planted in mass can achieve a "grove" effect. Proper use of mulches also goes hand in hand with mass plantings. Plants with mulch will require less water in the long run.

Edible plants are another attractive option to plant with separately or as a mass planting in a Xeriscape. Strawberries, carrots and lettuce all offer a different, yet beautiful texture to a landscape. They can be incorporated with plants of similar water needs or they can be planted in a separate area.

LIST OF PLANTS

The soil moisture estimates given in the following tables are based on the minimum water needs of established plants in clay loam type soils. A plant's soil moisture requirement will vary from location, type of soil and sun exposure. **Sandy soils may require more frequent watering than indicated.** Several plants listed have high soil moisture requirements, but even they have a place in a Xeriscape. There may be locations in the design such as a poorly drained low area or along the north side of the building, where these plants would be appropriate.

Since this book is written for Denver metro homeowners, plants are listed under the common name rather than the scientific name. The book's plant list is not intended to be all-inclusive. In fact, more and more low-water requiring plants are being discovered for use in Colorado each year. For more information about a particular plant or new plants that are not on this list, contact a local nursery or the local county's Colorado State University Cooperative Extension.

PLANT LIST LEGEND

Soil Moisture

- — — Exceptionally drought-enduring once established. No more than natural rainfall is needed.

- ○ — Dry, well-drained soils; two to three waterings per year; gauge the amount per watering by the reaction of the plant material.

- ◑ — Moist, well-drained soils; four to six waterings per year.

- ● — Moist, cool soils; never dry-these plants are good for poorly drained areas or north-facting locations

Sun Tolerance

* Full Shade
* Partial Shade
* Full Sun
  *Limited Plant Availability

Trees — Size in 40 Years

Small-Less than 25 ft.

Large-Greater than 25ft.

\# **Thorny —**
Has thorns or spikes; Aurora City Code prohibits the use of thorny or spiky plants on public right-of-way.

Plant List

Trees-Evergreen

Plant Name	Soil Moisture	Sun Tolerance	Size in 40 Years	Description and Comments
DOUGLAS FIR Pseudotsuga menziesii	◑	✳	(tree)	Loosely pyramidal in habit; bluegreen soft needle foliage; small bracted cones; tolerates poor soils; tolerates shade as well as sun and wind; best grown on dry side.
EASTERN REDCEDAR Juniperus virginiana	◐/-	☼	(tree)	Densely pyramidal or columnar; has scale-like foliage; female trees have blue berries; named varieties available; tolerant of wind and poor soil; slow to establish.
FIR, WHITE Abies concolor	●	✳✳☼	(tree)	Distinctly pyramidal; horizontal branching, blue-green, soft needled foliage; not tolerant of heavy clay soils; needs winter watering; growth rapid in comparison with other conifers; cones borne upright at tree's top.
JUNIPER, ONESEED Juniperus monosperma	-	✳☼	(tree)	Upright and dense; normally as wide as tall; from large shrub to small tree. Tolerates wide variety of soils and adverse conditions; slow to establish; can be difficult to find.
JUNIPER, ROCKY MOUNTAIN Juniperus scopulorum	-	☼	(tree)	Same as Eastern Redcedar, only Rocky Mountain Juniper is more cold hardy.
PINE, AUSTRIAN Pinus nigra	◐	✳☼	(tree)	Dark green leaves in bundles of two to 6½" long. Cones ¾" long; fast growing; dense; long-lived.
PINE, PONDEROSA Pinus ponderosa	◐	✳☼	(tree)	Dark green leaves in bundles of two; leaves to 6½" long; cones ¾" long; dense; long-lived; fast growing.
PINE, BRISTLECONE Pinus aristata	◐	✳☼	(tree)	Dark green, 1 - 1½" long leaves in bundles of five; dotted with droplets of resin; twisting, densely clothed branchlets under cultivation; long-lived.
PINE, LIMBER Pinus flexilis	◐	✳☼	(tree)	Dark green, 3" long leaves in bundles of five; stiff cones to 6" long; rounded open crown, branches often bare towards trunk; grey bark.
PINE, PINYON Pinus cembroides var. edulis	-	☼	(tree)	Dark green, 2" leaves in bundles of 2-3; cones globular to 2" long; edible nuts; prefers very well-drained site.

Plant Name	Soil Moisture	Sun Tolerance	Size in 40 Years	Description and Comments
PINE, SCOTS (Scotch) Pinue sylvestris	◇	☼	(tree)	Blue-green leaves that are stiff and twisted; 3″ long leaves in bundles of two; can assume rounded open crown or pyramdial; fast growing.
PINE, WHITE Pinus strobus	◆	✳ ☼	(tree)	Tall evergreen tree with soft green, graceful foilage; picturesque in older age due to later flattening at the top with occasional missing branches; 2-4″ needles in bundles of five; new needles are light green, very fine and flexible.
SPRUCE, BLACK HILLS Picea glauca cv. 'Densata'	●	✳ ☼	(tree)	A dense pyramidal tree; sharp needled foliage; tolerant of wide range of soils; very hardy in cold weather; resistant to salt conditions and snow accumulations; very slow growing. Can be difficult to find.
SPRUCE, COLORADO Picea pungens	●	✳ ☼	(tree)	Pyramidal shape; limbs to the ground; sharp-needled foliage; subject to winter desiccation but widely adaptable to most soils and conditions; silver blue varieties available.

Trees-Deciduous

Plant Name	Soil Moisture	Sun Tolerance	Size in 40 Years	Description and Comments
ASH, GREEN Fraxinus pennsylvanica var. lanceolata	◇ ◆	✳ ☼	(tree)	Compact oval crown; inconspicuous male and female flowers, on separate trees before leaves; seedless varieties are available; tolerates severe cold, wet, salty or poor soils; very hardy and drought tolerant.
ASH, WHITE Fraxinus americana	◇ ◆	✳ ☼	(tree)	Same as Green Ash.
ASH, EUROPEAN MOUNTAIN Sorbus aucuparia	◆	✳ ☼	(tree)	Oval to round crown; white blossoms in late spring followed by showy red-orange berries persisting into winter; attractive to birds; must have well-drained soil.
ASPEN, QUAKING Populus tremuloides	◆	✳ ☼	(tree)	White barked slender trunk; open, oval crown; long-stemmed triangular leaves always in motion; sprouts from underground rootstock; brillant yellow fall color; use in moist areas only; short-lived.

Plant Name	Soil Moisture	Sun Tolerance	Size in 40 Years	Description and Comments
BIRCH, CUTLEAF WEEPING Betula pendual cv. 'Gracilis'	◐	❄ ☼	🌳	White bark; pendulous branches and leaves; subject to insects/disease in hardship conditions; needs well drained soil; does not tolerate overwatering; avoid south and west exposures.
BLACK LOCUST* Robina pseudoacacia	○	❄ ☼	🌳	Open shape; fragrant white flowers early summer; red-brown seed pods persist into winter; subject to insect attack; adapted to poor soils.
BUCKEYE, OHIO* Aesculus glabra	○	❄ ☼	🌳	Round crown; upright panicles of white flowers in spring followed by nut; brillant orange fall color; slow to establish.
BUCKEYE, YELLOW Aesculus octandra	○	❄ ☼	🌳	Same as Ohio Buckeye.
CATALPA, WESTERN Catalpa speciosa	○	❄ ☼	🌳	Strong limbs; narrow silhouette; well adapted to the extremes of heat and cold; large white blossoms followed by bean-like seed pods.
CATALPA, CHINESE* Catalpa ovata	○	❄ ☼	🌳	Similar to above; flowers are yellow-white; smaller seed pods; not as hardy Western Catalpa.
CHERRY, EUROPEAN BIRD Prunus padus	○	❄ ☼	🌳	Open crown; first to unfurl leaves in spring; white fragrant flowers in early May; black cherry-like fruit.
CHOKECHERRY Prunus virginiana	◐	❄ ☼	🌳	Variable shape; red bark; clusters of white blossoms followed by red to black fruit that is attractive to birds; subject to insects and disease; orange fall color; leaves emerge green, turn and remain dark red throughout the summer; forms ticket.
CRABAPPLE, FLOWERING Malus spp.	◐	☼	🌳	Many varieties in different heights, flower colors and fruit colors; beautiful fall color; consult a local nurseryman for details.
ELM, SIBERIAN Ulmus pumila	●	❄ ☼	🌳	Rounded open crown; tolerant of poor soil; highly competitve root system; develops weak crotches if not pruned properly; poor fall color; subject to insect-attack.
GOLDEN RAINTREE Koelreuteria paniculata	○	❄ ☼	🌳	Flat open crown; yellow flowers in early summer; bladder-like seed pods persist into winter; yellow fall color; branches break in heavy snows.
HACKBERRY Celtis occidentalis	●	☼	🌳	Spreading round crown; tolerant of radiated heat, wind, wet, dry or alkaline soils; deep roots; will not heave sidewalks; yellow fall color; slow to establish.

Plant Name	Soil Moisture	Sun Tolerance	Size in 40 Years	Description and Comments
HAWTHORN Crataegus ssp.	◌ ◑	❋ ❋ ☼	🌳	Many varieties with different heights and different needs; thorns, white blossoms into late spring followed by red fruit persistent into winter that are attractive to birds; orange-scarlet fall color; Russian Hawthorn is the most drought tolerant variety.
HONEYLOCUST, THORNLESS Gleditsia triacanthos var. inermis	◌ ◑	❋ ☼	🌳	Round open crown; small leaflets give light shade; tolerant of acidic or salt conditions and severe cold; will withstand some drought conditions; yellow fall color.
HORSECHESTNUT* Aesculus hippocastanum	◑	❋ ☼	🌳	Round to pyramidal shape five-bladed leaves; upright flower clusters in May; spiny capsular fruits; nonfruiting form available; prefers rich moist soil; brown to yellow fall color.
KENTUCKY COFFEE TREE Gymnocladus diocius	◌	❋ ☼	🌳	Tall, upright tree with large open branches that are picturesque; many large pods often staying on until winter.
LILAC, JAPANESE TREE* Syringa japonica	◑	❋ ☼	🌳	Open crown; red bark; showy panicles of blossoms in summer.
LINDEN, AMERICAN Tilia americana	◑	❋ ❋ ☼	🌳	Dense, compact crown; heavy shade; slow to moderate growth; upright branching varieties available; good for formal areas.
LINDEN, LITTLELEAF Tilia cordata	◑	❋ ❋ ☼	🌳	Same as American Linden, but looks like a stiff, narrow tree with small leaves.
MAPLE, BIGTOOTH Acer grandidentatum	◑	❋ ☼	🌳	Rounded crown; three lobed leaves; rose to red fall color; can be pruned into a shrub or tree.
MULBERRY, WHITE* Morus alba	◌	❋ ☼	🌳	Round topped, spreading dense tree. Female trees have berries that will stain and may be messy.
NEW MEXICO LOCUST Robinia neo-mexicana	◌	☼	🌳	Suckering pattern; fragrant pink flowers in early summer; small seed pods persist throughout winter; yellow fall color.
OAK, BUR Quercus macrocarpa	◌	❋ ☼	🌳	Large, irregular tree with rugged, picturesque form in maturity. Large, glossy green leaves; may be messy; likes clay soils.
OAK, ENGLISH Quercus robur	◑	☼	🌳	May be pruned to create a short trunk with broad spreading branches and wide open crown; moderate growth, holds leaves into winter.
OAK, NORTHERN RED Quercus rubra	◑	❋ ❋ ☼	🌳	Broad, spreading branches; high branching shape; deep root system; new leaves and leaf stalks red in spring and turn a dark red in fall; does not tolerate clay soils.

Plant Name	Soil Moisture	Sun Tolerance	Size in 40 Years	Description and Comments
OAK, GAMBEL OR SCRUB Quercus gambelli	◐ (low)	❋ ☼	🌳	Short trunk; though scaled bark; drought tolerant; may form many trunks; orange fall color; may be pruned into small tree or shrub.
OAK, SWAMP WHITE Quercus bicolor	◐ (low)	☼	🌳	Narrow silhouette; round top; dense foliage; yellow to red-brown fall color.
PEAR, CALLERY Pyrus calleryana	◕	❋ ☼	🌳	Dense pyramidal shape with strong horizontal branching. Small, inedible fruit. Early, white spring flower clusters and wine red to scarlet late fall color; many varieties available with a variety of different forms.
PEAR, USSURIAN Pyrus ussuriensis	◑	❋ ☼	🌳	Dense pyramidal shape with strong horizontal branching. Brillant, red fall foliage; inedible fruit.
PLUM, WILD Prunus americana	◐ (low)	❋ ☼	🌳	Aromatic white flowers before leaves early spring during alternative years; yellow fruits; green, serated foliage; gray bark; yellow fall color; may form a thicket; may be pruned into a shrub or tree.
PLUM, NEWPORT Prunus bilirieana cv. 'Newport'	◐ (low)	❋ ☼	🌳	Red-purple spring foliage changing to green-white flowers; red stamens; seldom fruits.
REDBUD, EASTERN Cercis canadensis	◕	❋ ❋	🌳	Round head; horizontally tiered branches; pink flowers in early spring are flat seed pods persisting into winter; yellow fall color; may be pruned into a multi-stem shrub or small tree.
RUSSIAN OLIVE Elaeagnus angustifolia	-	☼	🌳	Small tree with silver gray leaves; brown shedding bark; small, olive-like berries and crowded twisted trunk. Adaptable to shrub or tree form by pruning; adapatable to just about any soil; very hardy and drought tolerant; attractive to wildlife.
SYCAMORE, AMERICAN Plantanus occidentalis	◕	❋ ☼	🌳	Tall shade tree with large maple-like leaves; bark sheds in patches to reveal pale, smooth, new bark underneath; brown ball-like seed clusters attractive in winter; becomes greenish-yellow in alkaline soils.
TREE OF HEAVEN Ailanthus altissima	◐ (low)	☼	🌳	Large divided leaves that have an odor when crushed; root suckers unless soil is kept dry; excellent red-orange-yellow fall color; can be messy.

Shrubs-Deciduous and Evergreen

Plant Name	Soil Moisture	Sun Tolerance	Maximum Height (ft.)	Description and Comments
AGAVE, UTAH Agave utahensis	-	✹ ☼	10	Cold hardy; evergreen rosettes of fleshy leaves; 6 to 10 feet tall flowering stalk; several years to bloom.
ALTHEA (ROSE OF SHARON) Hibiscus syriacus	◐	✹ ☼	10	White, red and purple flowers in July and August; large showy, hollyhock-like flowers.
APACHE PLUME Fallugia paradoxa	-	✹ ☼	6	White stems; finely cut foliage; flowers and silky seed plumes all summer; 1½" white flowers in spring.
ASH, SINGLELEAF Fraxinus anomala	-	☼	25	Multi-stemmed small tree or large shrub; single, oval-shaped deciduous leaves make this ash unlike all others; yellow fall color.
ASH, WAFER Ptelea trifoliata	○	☼	18	Several varieties with straight or crooked stems; wafer-fruits in late summer; yellow fall color.
BARBERRY, JAPANESE # Berberis thunbergi	○	✹ ☼	4	Small, spatula-like leaves; thorny; var. 'Atropurpurea' is purple-leaved.
BARBERRY, MENTOR # Berberis mentorensis	○	✹ ☼	4	Hybrid of the above; semi-evergreen foliage; armed with 1" spines; good barrier plant.
BARBERRY, CRIMSON PYGMY # Berberis thunberfi cv. 'Crimson Pygmy'	○	✹ E. Exp.	3	Not showy; compact, reddish-purple foliage
BEAUTYBUSH Kolkwitzia amabilis	◐	✹ ☼	10	Profuse pink flowers on gracefully arched branches; withstands reflected heat; suckers from base; needs watering in dry years.
BITTERBRUSH, ANTELOPE Purshia tridentata	-	✹ ☼	4	Leaves three-cut at tip; tolerates alkaline soils; ¾-1" yellow flowers; interesting color and texture.
BLADDERSENNA, COMMON* Colutea arborescens	○	✹ ☼	5	Yellow May flowers; an inflated "bladder-like" fruit which persist into winter.
BLUEBEARD, BLUEMIST Spirea Caryopteris x clandonensis	◐	✹ ☼	4	Semi-herbaceous; late summer spikes of blue flowers; gray-green foliage; cut back in spring; winter seed heads attractive.

Plant Name	Soil Moisture	Sun Tolerance	Maximum Height (ft.)	Description and Comments
BROOM, WARMINSTER Cytisus x praecox	◒	☀ ☼	3	Lemon-yellow flowers in May on nearly leafless, dark green, slender stems; stem stay greenish all winter.
BUCKTHORN, COMMON # Rhamnus cathartica	◒	☀ ☼	20	May be pruned to be tree-like; spines; inconspicuous flowers; black-berries on female; indifferent as to soils; good barrier hedge.
BUCKTHORN, COLUMNAR Rhamnus frangula cv. 'Tallhedge'	◐	☀ ☼	20	Useful as a screen planting.
BUCKTHORN, SMITH Rhamnus smithii	◒	☼	9	Round-shaped, deciduous shrub wtih ½" long green or inconspicuous flowers; yellow fall color.
BUFFALOBERRY* Shepherdia argentea	All	☀ ☼	18	Silvery foliage and stems; red fruit on female; found natively only along streams; may adapt to any type of soil mositure.
BUTTERFLYBUSH, FOUNTAIN Buddleia alternifolia	◒	☀ ☼	8	Dense cluster of lilac flowers on long, gracefully arching branches in mid-May.
BUTTERFLYBUSH, ORANGE-EYE Buddleia davidi	◒	☀ ☼	12	Purple, magenta or white flowers on upright plant in August; cut back in the spring; very attractive to butterflies; dies to the ground in winter.
CEANOTHUS FENDLERI Ceanothus fendleri	◒	☀ ☼	2	Deciduous, loosely-branched small shrub; dark green elliptic leaves; clusters of fragrant white blossoms in the spring; no fall color; thicker in full sunlight.
CHERRY, CISTENA (PLUM) Prunus cistena	◐	☀	5	Pink May flowers; reddish-purple leaves.
CHERRY, NANKING Prunus tomentosa	◒	☀ ☼	8	Single white flowers before leaves in late April; showy red, edible fruit; great for birds.
CHERRY, PURPLELEAF Prunus x cistena	◐	☀ ☼	5	Hybrid sand cherry with red foliage; white flowers in early May.
CHERRY, PIN Prunus pennsylvanica	◒	☼	8	Somewhat suckering deciduous shrub; pink to white spring flowers in clusters; brightly colored fall leaf colors; pea-sized edible red cherries.
CHERRY, SAND Prunus besseyi	◒	☀ ☼	5	Narrow, lance-like foliage, native; likes sandy soils; black, edible, tasty fruit; useful for wildlife cover.
CHOKECHERRY Prunus virginiana	◒ ◐	☀ ☼	18	Coarse shrub to small tree with "chains" of white May flowers, followed by black edible fruit; suckers easily.
CINQUEFOIL (POTENTILLA) Potentilla fruiticosa	◐	☀ ☼	4	Yellow flowers in mid-May and through early summer; many varieties are available; popular with homeowners.

Plant Name	Soil Moisture	Sun Tolerance	Maximum Height (ft.)	Description and Comments
CLIFFROSE Cowania stansburiana	●	✸ ☼	3	Yellow to white flowers; small evergreen leaves; open, irregular form.
CORALBERRY, CHENAULT Symphoricarpos x chenaulti	-	✸ ✸ ☼	5	Small pink flower; upright shrub arching under the coral red berries that persist through winter; good for slopes and shade.
CORALBERRY, HANCOCK Symphoricarpos orbiculatus cv. Hancock	◔	✸ ☼	1½	Pink flowers; low growing shrub used as a groundcover or for erosion control on slopes; tiny pink flowers followed by rose-pink berries. Hardy to 7500 ft.
CORALBERRY, INDIAN CURRANT Symphoricarpos orbiculatus	◔	✸ ☼	4	Native; loose open shape; grayish-green leaves; whitish-pink flowers in June; followed by small clusters of purple-red fruit maturing in September and October.
CORNELIAN CHERRY Cornus mas	◑	✸ ☼	10	Yellow flowers in March or early April; scarlet, cherry-like edible fruit.
COTONEASTER, CRANBERRY Cotoneaster apiculata	◔	✸ ☼	3	More wide than tall; glossy leaves; large, showy, red berries persist in winter.
COTONEASTER, FLOWERING Cotoneaster multiflora	◔	✸ ☼	8	Broad-spreading; loose clusters of white flowers; pink berries; orange fall color.
COTONEASTER PEKING Cotoneaster acutifolia	◔	✸ ☼	6	Upright-spreading; pink flower clusters; black fruit.
COTONEASTER, ROCK Cotoneaster horizontalis	◔	✸ ☼	4	Wider than tall; glossy leaves; almost evergreen; showy red berries persisting into winter.
COTONEASTER, SMALL-LEAVED Cotoneaster microphylla	◑	E. Exp.	3	White flowers in June; tiny leaves and red fruit.
COTONEASTER, SPREADING Cotoneaster divaricata	◔	☼	5	Pink May flowers; red fruit.
CURRANT, ALPINE Ribes alpinum	◑	✸ ☼	5	Glossy green foliage; male plant has red, edible fruit; bronze fall color; good hedge plant.
CURRANT, GOLDEN Ribes aureum	● ◑ ◔	✸ ☼	6	Arching branches; showy yellow flowers in mid-May; red to black edible fruit; underground suckers; red fall color.
CURRANT, SQUAW Ribes cereum	◔	☼	3	Much-branched spineless deciduous shrub; greenish-white to fragrant flowers in early summer, followed by delicious red berries; yellow fall color.

Plant Name	Soil Moisture	Sun Tolerance	Maximum Height (ft.)	Description and Comments
ELAEAGNUS OR OLIVE, AUTUMN Elaeagnus umbellata	◊	☀ ☼	18	Gray-green foliage; fragrant yellow flowers in mid-May; silvery and brown fruit that turns red in fall.
ELDER, AMERICAN Sambucus canadensis	◐	☀ ☼	10	Arching stems with showy white, flat clusters of flowers in late June; edible blackberries in late summer.
EUONYMUS, EASTERN* Euonymus atropurpureus	◐	☀ ☼	10	Stiffly upright; bright red fall color; pink to orange fruit.
EUONYMUS, WINGED Euonymus alatus	◊ ◐	☀ ☼	6	Bright crimson fall color; twiggy branches often with four corky ridges; scarlet fruit; must have well-drained soil.
EUONYMUS, EUROPEAN Euonymus europaeus	◐	E. Exp.	12	Yellow May flowers; red fall color and red fruit.
EUONYMUS, SARCOXIE Euonymus fortunei cv. 'Sarcoxie'	◐	☀	8	Broadleaf evergreen to semi-evergreen; best in north or east exposure.
FERNBUSH Chamaebatiaria millefolium	-	☼	5	Semi-evergreen, sticky, aromatic leaves that resemble fern leaves; large showy clusters of fragrant white flowers in mid-summer.
FIRE THORN Pyracantha coccinea	◊	E. Exp.	8	Small clusters of white flowers in mid-June; orange-red fruit; vars. 'Wyatti' and 'Pauciflora' are hardiest; semi-evergreen.
FORSYTHIA Forsythia intermedia	◊ ◐	☼	10	Yellow April flowers; vars. 'Farrand' and 'Lynwood Gold' are the most showy.
GOOSEBERRY, SLENDER-FLOWERED # Ribes leptanthum	◊	☼	4	Erect, bristly shrub with dark green leaves; tiny greenish-white flowers in late spring.
GOOSEBERRY, WHITESTEM # Ribes inerme	◊	☀ ☼	5	White arching stems; not showy flowers; large black edible berries; stiff thorns.
GRAPEHOLLY, OREGON Mahonia aquifolium	◊ ◐	☀ ☼ N. or E. Exp.	6	Fragrant, yellow flowers in early May; glossy, evergreen foliage.
HEAVENLY BAMBOO* Nandina domestica	◐	☀ ☼ E. Exp.	3	Brillant red fall color.
HONEYSUCKLE, AMUR Lonicera maacki	◐	☀ ☼	15	Its very fragrant flowers change from white to yellow; flowers bloom in late May; usually a heavy crop of dark red berries in fall.

Plant Name	Soil Moisture	Sun Tolerance	Maximum Height (ft.)	Description and Comments
HONEYSUCKLE, BLUELEAF Lonicera korolkowi	◊ ◗	✳ ☼	10	Rose-red, early spring flowers; blue-green foliage; red to orange-red fruit in mid-summer.
HONEYSUCKLE, TATARIAN Lonicera tatarica	◊ ◗	✳ ☼	12	Pink to creamy white flowers; similar in other respects to Blueleaf honeysuckle.
INDIGOBUSH Amorpha fruticosa	◗	✳	5	Purple spikes in summer; green foliage; best as a background.
JUNIPER, PFITZER Juniperus chinensis cv. 'Pfitzer'	◊ ●	✳ ☼	8	Evergreen, scale-like foliage; spreading to 21"; good windbreak.
JUNIPER, ARMSTRONG GLOBE Juiperus chinensis cv. 'Armstrong'	◊ ●	☼	4	Evergreen; popular globe form for formal effect. Many other varieties of junipers are available.
LEADPLANT Amorpha canescens	◗	☼	4	Purple spikes in summer; gray-green foliage.
LILAC, CHINESE* Syringa x chinensis	◊ ●	✳ ☼	6	Purple flower panciles; strong arching stems; no fall color.
LILAC, COMMON Syringa vulgaris	◊ ●	✳ ☼	8	Fragrant purple flowers in early May; grafted forms in white, pink, magenta and deep purple; suckers at base; no fall color.
LILAC, LATE* Syringa villosa	◊ ●	✳ ☼	8	Rosy-lilac to white flowers in early June; one of the hardiest; no fall color.
LILAC, MEYER'S Syringa meyeri	◊	✳ ☼	7	Dense shrub with small spikes of dark purple flowers in early June.
LILAC, PERSIAN Syringa x persica	◊ ●	✳ ☼	8	Profusely but loosely flowered shrub; lavender flowers in June; seldoms suckers from base.
LILAC, MacFARLANE Syringa reflexa	◊	✳ ☼	6	Pink flowers in late May; blooms later than common lilac.
MANZANITA, GREENLEAF Arctostaphylos patula	◊	✳ ☼	4	Broadleaf evergreen with circular to oval-shaped leathery leaves; clusters of pink to white urn-shaped flowers in spring followed by green turning to red or brown berries in fall.

Plant Name	Soil Moisture	Sun Tolerance	Maximum Height (ft.)	Description and Comments
MAPLE, AMUR Acer amur	◐	☀ ☼	18	Rounded shape; large shrub or multi-stemmed tree; red fall color.
MAPLE, ROCKY MOUNTAIN Acer glabrum	◐	☀ ☼	18	Rounded shape; large shrub or multi-stemmed small tree; slender stems with winter-red buds; yellow to reddish-orange fall color; quick growing.
MOCKORANGE Philadelphus ssp.	◐	☀ ☼	6	White, fragrant, single or double flowers in late May to mid-June; lower stems often bare; best in background.
MOCKORANGE, FALSE* Fendlera rupicola	◌	☀ ☼	5	Single, twisted leaves; white or tinged rose flowers in May; thrives under the hottest, dry conditions.
MOCKORANGE, LITTLELEAF Philadelphus microphyllus	◌	☼	6	Deciduous, freely-branching, ascending shrub with a rounded shape; reddish-brown bark shreds into thin strips; lemon-scented white blossoms into late spring; yellow-green fall color.
MORMON TEA, GREEN Ephedra viridis	-	☼	4	Evergreen stems with insignificant leaves; bright yellow flowers in spring; tea made from stems.
MORMON TEA, TORREY Ephedra torreyana	-	☼	2	Distinctly blue stems; bright yellow flowers in the spring; insignificant leaves; slow growing.
MOUNTAIN LOVER Paxistima myrsinites	-	☼	20	Evergreen shrub for permanent full shade or partial shade; small dark leaves; inconspicuous flowers; with time will sucker to form a groundcover.
MOUNTAIN MAHOGANY, COMMON Cercocarpus montanus	-	☀ ☼	6	Not showy flowers; fruit with silky, curly "tail".
MOUNTAIN MAHOGANY, CURL-LEAF Cercocarpus ledifolius	-	☀ ☼	12	Evergreen; narrow and often curled leaves; Grey-green color; interesting growth.
MOUNTAIN MAHOGANY, LITTLELEAF Cercocarpus intricatus	-	☼	4	Multi-branched upright shrub covered with tiny ½" or less long evergreen, leathery leaves; inconspicuous flowers; slow growing but with a dense, branching habit.
NINEBARK, COMMON Physocarpus opulifolius	◌ ◐	☀ ☼	6	Small-lobed foliage; white to pink flowers in early June; reddish to brown fruit; red fall color.
NINEBARK, MOUNTAIN Physocarpus monogynus	◌ ◐	☀ ☼	6	Arching stems; brown shedding bark; white, short-lived flower clusters; prefers shade; orange fall color.

Plant Name	Soil Moisture	Sun Tolerance	Maximum Height (ft.)	Description and Comments
NOLINA, TEXAS Nolina texana	-	☼	3	Flowers are tiny but bunched by the hundreds on a 2-3' spike; 1"-2" wide arching, leathery evergreen leaves; slow growing.
PEASHRUB, LITTLE-LEAF Caragana microphylla	-	✵☼	5	Tiny leaves in bundles of fours; yellow flowers in late spring.
PEASHRUB, PYGMY Caragana pygmaea	-	☼	3	Yellow May flowers; useful as a low hedge.
PEASHRUB, SIBERIAN Caragana arborescens	-	☼	18	Yellow May flowers; makes a good screen or windbreak.
PINE, MUGO Pinus mugo	◌	✵ ☼	20	Evergreen; dwarf to tree size available; shrubby; 1"-2" long cones; several varieties available; deer eat this pine regularly.
PRIVET, AMUR Ligustrum amurense	◌	✵ ☼	8	Fragrant, tiny white flowers in June; dull blackberries; commonly used as a hedge.
PRIVET, NEW MEXICO Forestiera neomexicana	-	✵ ☼	8	Not a true privet; yellow flowers in early spring; male plants most showy; female plants' fruit dull blue-black; attractive cream color bark; upright form.
PRIVET, REGEL # Lingustrum regelianum	◌	✵☼	6	Not showy flowers; black fruits.
QUINCE, FLOWERING* Chaenomeles speciosa	◌	✵☼	6	Showy flowers in April and May; colors vary from scarlet to pink, white and variegated; pear-like, hard fruit that is useful for pectin content.
RABBITBRUSH, GREEN RUBBER Chrysothamnus nauseosus ssp. graveoleus	-	☼	4	The common rabbitbrush of the plains; multiple upright evergreen branches; plumes of golden flowers in late summer; no significant fall color; large showy clusters of fragrant white flowers in mid-summer. There are attractive dwarf varieties available, as well as gray and green stem varieties.
RABBITBRUSH, BLUE RUBBER Chrysothamnus nauseosus ssp. nauseosus	-	☼	4	Slightly less common than Green Rabbitbrush; blue evergreen branches; plumes of golden yellow flowers in late summer; plants of three in mass: fast growing.
RASPBERRY, BOULDER Rubus deliciosus	◌	✵	5	Large white, solitary flowers in late May; dark fruit.
ROSE, AUSTRIAN COPPER # Rosa foetida cv. 'Bicolor'	◌	☼	6	Coppery-red and yellow flowers; often mixed colors on same plant; a rambly, vine-like growth habit.

Plant Name	Soil Moisture	Sun Tolerance	Maximum Height (ft.)	Description and Comments
ROSE, FATHER HUGO # Rosa hugonis	◌	✹ ☼	6	Profuse canary-yellow, 2″ flowers in late May; arching shrub.
ROSE, HARISON'S YELLOW # Rosa x harisonii	◌	✹ ☼	6	Profuse, yellow flowers in early June; thorns.
ROSE, REDLEAF # Rosa rubrifolia	◌	✹ ✹	6	Sparse, pink blooms in early June; reddish foliage.
ROSE, SHRUB # Rosa rugosa	◌	✹ ☼	5	Pink to white blooms in early June; showy brick red-orange; orange fall color.
ROSE, PERSIAN YELLOW # Rosa foetida cv. 'Perisiana'	◌	☼	6	Doubled, yellow flowers in May-June; graceful arching shrub.
ROSE, WOODS # Rosa woodsii	◌	☼	9	Prostrate to upright shrub; light pink to deep rose flowers .4-1″ petals; blooms late spring through summer; a hip fruit that is persistent through the winter; some spread by root sprouting.
SAGEBRUSH, BASIN BIG* Artemisia tridentata ssp. tridentata	-	☼	6	Gray-blue evergreen leaves are aromatic when crushed; single to several stems.
SAGE, BIG Artemisia tridentata	-	☼	8	Evergreen, aromatic leaves; the most widespread and numerous shrub of the west; very fragrant; blue-gray foliage.
SAGE, FRINGED Artemisia frigida	-	✹ ☼	2	Gray-green foliage; aromatic; evergreen basal leaves; may form a soft dense mat.
SAGEBRUSH, SAND Artemisia filifolia	-	☼	3	Soft, silvery-white, needle-fine, aromatic leaves; native to sandy soils; single to several stems.
SAGEBRUSH, WYOMING Artemisia tridentata ssp. wyomingensis	-	☼	3	Uneven flot-topped shrub with aromatic, gray-blue, evergreen leaves; adapts to shallower and leaner soils better than Basin Big Sagebrush.
SALTBUSH, FOURWING* Artiplex canescens	-	☼	5	High salt-tolerant; light-grey leaves; attracts wildlife; coarse texture.
SEA BUCKTHORN Hippophae rhamnoides	-	✹ ☼	8	Silvery, narrow foliage in densely-branched pattern; female plant's orange-red fruit is persistent into the winter; useful for saline soils.
SERVICEBERRY Amelanchier alnifolia	◌	✹ ☼	10	Small toothed leaves; white flowers in May; prefers rocky, well-drained site; orange fall color; edible fruits.

Plant Name	Soil Moisture	Sun Tolerance	Maximum Height (ft.)	Description and Comments
SILVERBERRY* Elaeagnus commutata	○	☽ ☼	6	Silvery foliage; silvery berry attracts birds.
SNOWBERRY Symphoricarpus albus	○ ●	☽	5	Small pink blooms in mid-June; showy, white fruit into late fall.
SPIREA, BRIDAL WREATH Spirea prunifolia cv. 'Plena'	●	☽ ☼	5	Profuse, double, white flowers in May.
SPIREA, FROEBEL Spirea x bumalda cv. 'Froebelii'	●	☽ ☼	3	Lavender flowers in June; does not tolerate highly-alkaline soils.
SPIREA, SNOWMOUND Spirea nipponica	●	☽ ☼ E. Exp.	5	Profuse, white flowers in May; graceful, arching.
SPIREA, ROCK Holodiscus dumosus	○	☼	4	Deciduous, upright shrub with ¾-1" long leaves; sprays of white to pink flowers persisting when dry, turning russet color; russet fall color; spicy odor to crushed leaves; moderate grower.
SPIREA, VANHOUTTE Spiraea vanhouttei	●	☽ ☼	6	White flowers in May; an old-fashioned favorite; arching.
SPRUCE, MAXWELL* Picea abies cv. 'Maxwellii'	●	N. or E. Exp.	3	Slow-growing; forms mound twice as broad as high; evergreen.
SQUAW APPLE Peraphyllum ramosissimum	○	☼	8	Upright, rigidly-branched deciduous shrub; pink spring flowers followed by small, fleshly, edible fruit; russet brown fall color.
SUMAC, MOUNTAIN OR DWARF SMOOTH Rhus glabra var. cismontana	●	☼	3	Greenish flowers in May; brillant scarlet fall color; red cone-like fruit; spreading from root sprouts; attracts birds.
SUMAC, SMOOTH Rhus glabra	○	☽ ☼	15	Glossy, fern-like foliage; deep red fruit clusters at tips of branches persisting into winter; red fall color.
SUMAC, STAGHORN Rhus typhina	○	☽ ☼	15	Similar to smooth sumac, but branches are covered with velvety hairs; bright red fall color; the dwarf, cut-leaf var. 'laciniata' is popular for the "ferny" appearance.
SUMAC, THREELEAF Rhus trilobata	-	☽ ☼	4	Glossy, 3-leaved foliage; yellow flowers in early May; red fruit; aromatic; native; bright orange fall color.
TOMATILLO Lycium pallidum	-	☼	4	Deciduous shrub with stiff, gently arching branches; greenish-white to purplish tubular flowers in early summer, followed by orange edible fruits; yellow fall color.

Plant Name	Soil Moisture	Sun Tolerance	Maximum Height (ft.)	Description and Comments
VIBURNUM, EUROPEAN CRANBERRY Viburnum opulus	◐	☀ ☼	10	White flowers in flat clusters in May; red fruit; yellow-fruited and dwarf forms available.
VIBURNUM, ARROWWOOD* Viburnum dentatum	◐	☀	5	Creamy white flat clusters of flowers in early June; black fruit; glossy red fall color.
VIBURNUM, BURKWOOD Viburnum burkwoodii	◐	E. Exp.	4	Pinkish to white flowers in May; shiny foliage.
VIBURNUM, KOREAN-SPICE Viburnum carlesii	◐	E. Exp.	4	Pinkish-white, spicy-fragrant flowers in May.
VIBURNUM, NANNYBERRY Viburnum lentago	◌ ◐	☀ ☼	15	Tall shrub or small tree; flowers in white flat clusters; black fruit; purple-red fall color.
VIBURNUM, WAYFARINGTREE Viburnum lantana	- ◌	☀ ☼	8	White flowers in flat clusters in mid-May; gray-green foliage; suckers at base; raisin-like fruit in winter.
WINTERFAT Eurotia lanata	-	☼	2	Silver-green foliage; turns creamy beige in fall; native; best in clay soils.
YUCCA, ADAMSNEEDLE # Yucca filamentosa	-	S	1½	Wide, evergreen foliage; stiff upright rosettes from base; white flowers in spikes.
YUCCA, BANANA # Yucca baccata	-	☼	3	Stout, almost fleshy, broad, evergreen leaves; predominantly white lily-like flowers in summer; fruit resembles fat banana and can be eaten as well as roasted; green and blue-green leaved varieties available.
YUCCA, SOAPTREE # Yucca elata	-	☼	15	Slender, evergreen leaves; lily-like white flowers on very tall stalk.
YUCCA, SOAPWEED # Yucca glauca	-	☀ ☼	6	Narrow, evergreen foliage; stiff upright rosettes from base; white flowers in upright spikes.
WILLOW, BLUE STEM Salix irrorata	◐ ●	☀ ☼	6	Blue-gray stems and red leaves in early winter; narrow foliage; male plant has black winter buds, opening to silvery catkins in early spring.

a)

b)

c)

a) Flowering Crabapple
    Malus spp.
    Aurora Forestry Division

b) Western Catalpa
    Catalpa speciosa
    Aurora Forestry Division

c) Golden Raintree
    Koelreuteria paniculata
    Aurora Forestry Division

Austrian Pine
Pinus nigra
Aurora Forestry Division

a)

b)

c)

Mugo Pine
Pinus mugo
Aurora Forestry Division

Woods Rose
Rosa woodsii
Alan Rollinger

a)   Himalayan Border Jewel
     Polygonum affine
     Alan Rollinger

b)   Serviceberry
     Amelanchier alnifolia
     Alan Rollinger

c)   Native Chokecherry
     Prunus virginiana
     Alan Rollinger

Pineleaf Penstemon
Penstemon pinifolius
Alan Rollinger

Crocus
Crocus spp.
Ken Ball

a)

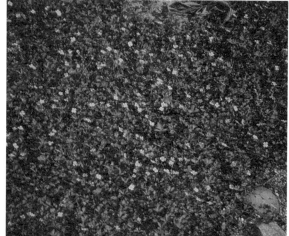

b)

c)

a)   Paperflower, Golden
     Zinnia grandiflora
     Alan Rollinger

b)   Creeping potentilla
     Potentilla verna nana
     Aurora Utilities Department

c)   Rocky Mountain Penstemon
     Penstemon strictus var. 'Bandera'
     Ken Ball

a)

b)

c)

a) Lavender Cotton
Santolina chamaecyparissus
Alan Rollinger

b) Purple Iceplant
Delosperma cooperi
Ken Ball

c) Oregon Grape Holly, Creeping
Mahonia repens
Ken Ball

Yellow Hardy Iceplant
Delosperma nubigenum
Alan Rollinger

a) This homeowner reduced the amount of water needed for his backyard by placing flowering groundcovers.
Denver Water Department

b) This slope is covered with a selection of low-water groundcovers and perennials.
Ken Ball

c) Sunroses, evergreens and a wooden walkway make this a low-watering requiring landscape wonder.
Alan Rollinger

a)

b)

c)

These low-water requiring California poppies are keeping this slope beautiful without requiring a lot of maintenance or mowing.
Denver Water Department

Perennials

Plant Name	Soil Moisture	Sun Tolerance	Description and Comments
ASTERS, NEW YORK Aster novi-belgii	◐	☼	12-16" tall; purple-white flowers.
BACHELOR'S BUTTON, PERENNIAL Centaurea montana	◯	☼	18" height and 24" spread; brillant blue flowers in spring.
BASKET OF GOLD Alyssum saxatile	◐	☼	6-8" in height and 12" in spread; early spring yellow bloom.
BABY'S BREATH, CREEPING Gypsophila repens	◯	☼	2" in height and 8" in depth; fragile looking with white flowers.
BEEBALM Monarda didyma	◐	☼	18" in height; aggressive spreader; light purple flower.
BLANKET FLOWER Gaillardia aristata	◯	☼	18" in height and 24" in spread; yellow and orange flowers all season.
BUTTER AND EGGS Linaria vulgaris	◐	☼	15" in height, yellow snapdragon-like flowers in early summer; very aggressive spreader; good for slopes; great in mountains.
BUTTERFLY WEED Ascelpias tuberosa	◯	☼	15" in height and spread; bright orange flowers in mid-summer.
CANDYTUFT, EVERGREEN Iberis sempervirens	◐	☼	1-6"; blue flowers.
CHOCOLATE FLOWER Berlandiera lyrata	-	☼	12-16" tall; yellow flowers with green centers; distinct chocolate aroma.
CINQUEFOIL, HORSE Potentilla hippiana	-	☼	8-12" tall; silvery leaves with sprays of golden yellow blossoms during mid-summer.
CONEFLOWER, PRAIRIE Ratibida columnifera	-	☼	12-14" tall; 1-1½" yellow to yellow and red brown daisy-like flowers in June till August.
CONEFLOWER, PURPLE Echinacea purpurea	◯	☼	30" in height and 36" in spread; soft lavender flowers, purple, pink and white cultivars available.
COTTAGE PINKS Dianthus plumarius	◯	☼	3-8"; red, white and pink flowers in May and June; many other species and cultivars available.

Plant Name	Soil Moisture	Sun Tolerance	Description and Comments
COREOPSIS Coreopsis sp.	◌	☼	Wide variety of heights are available; bright golden-yellow flowers throughout the summer.
CROCUS Crocus spp.	◌	☼	To 3″ tall; this popular multi-colored group of spring bulbs requires very little water to thrive.
DAISY, CUT-LEAF Erigeron compositus	◌	☼	2-6″ tall; evergreen mounds with 1″ wide white, blue or pink blossoms; very early spring blooming.
DAISY, BLACKFOOT Melampodium leucanthum	-	☼	6-12″ tall; creamy white flowers smother the plant from June to frost.
DAYLILIES Hemerocallis spp.	◌	❀☼	Wide variety of sizes, colors and season of bloom.
FLAX, BLUE Linum perenne	◌	☼	Small blue flowers periodically throughout the summer; great for a meadow or wildflower look; aggressive spreader.
FLAX, YELLOW Linum flavum	◌	☼	Vivid yellow flowers in early to mid-summer; more formal-looking than blue flax and not as tough.
FOUR-O'CLOCK, COLORADO Mirabilis multiflora	-	☼	12-24″ tall and wide; prostate stems with leathery leaves; magenta flowers open in early evening and remain open till mid-morning.
GAY FEATHER, DOTTED Liatris punctata	◌	☼	Spikes of tiny lavender flowers; 18-24″ in spread and in height.
GOLDEN MARGUERITE Anthemis tinctoria	◌	☼	12″ high; 12-15″ tall; bright yellow flowers with fern-like grey foliage; often acts as a biennial.
GRAPE HYACINTH Muscari botryoides	◌	☼	4-6″ tall; this familar and fragrant, blue-purple spring flower needs little water; multiplies rapidly.
HAREBELL Campanula rotundifolia	◌	☼	6-12″ tall; nodding blue-bell flowers from June to July.
HAREBELL, CARPATHIAN Campanula carpatica	◑	☼	4-6″; blue-lilac flowers.
INDIAN PAINTBRUSH, WHOLELEAF Castilleja integra	-	☼	4-12″ tall; brillant orange-red flowers in May through August.
LAVENDER COTTON Santolina chamaecyparissus	◌	☼	12-15″ high, yellow button bloom; mid to late summer; evergreen, aromatic, grey foliage.

Plant Name	Soil Moisture	Sun Tolerance	Description and Comments
LUPINE, SILVERY Lupinus argenteus	-	☼	20-40″ tall; deep blue-purple flowers from June to August.
MALLOW, PURPLE POPPY Callirhoe involucrata	-	☼	Ground-hugging, vine-like form; 1½-2″ brillant purple-red flowers, from June to August.
MORNING-GLORY, BUSH Ipomoea leptophylla	-	☼	1′-4′ tall and wide; large, bush-like, long-lived perennial; 3″-4″ wide rose-red flowers; will not spread; likes sandy soils; mid to late blooming.
PAPERFLOWER, GOLDEN Zinnia grandiflora	-	☼	Long-lasting yellow bloom; 6″ high and 12″ in spread.
PASQUE FLOWER Anemone pulsatilla	◌	☼	1′ in height; blue-lavender flowers in April and May.
PENSTEMON, FLAT-FACED (PHLOX) Penstemon ambigus	◌	☼	Phlox-like flower; 18″ tall; pink blush blossoms in July, August and September.
PENSTEMON, NARROW LEAVED Penstemon angustifolius	◌	☼	6-18″ tall; stiff upright stems with sky-blue snapdragon-like blossoms in May and June; likes sandy soils.
PENSTEMON, PINELEAF Penstemon pinifolius	◌	☼	6-10″ tall, evergreen pine-like leaves; orange-red blossoms in June and July; some groundcover qualities.
PENSTEMON, ROCKY MOUNTAIN Penstemon strictus var. 'Bandera'	◌	☼	Blue flowers late June; 24″ high; evergreen glossy foliage.
PENSTEMON, SHELL-LEAF Penstemon grandiflorus	◌	☼	To 3′ tall; blue-green shell-shaped foliage; tall flowering stems with large pale-purple to pink blossoms in May and June.
PENSTEMON, SIDEBELLS Penstemon secundiflorus	◌	☼	8-18″ tall; deep green leaves; upright stalks with pink to lavender to deep-blue blossoms in May to June; short-lived.
POPPY, ICELAND Papaver nudicavle	◑	☼	Blooms all summer long; add mulch to the soil; does well in the mountains.
POPPY, PRICKLY Argemone hispida	-	☼	12-24″ tall; prickly blue-green foliage; 3″-4″ wide white poppy-like flowers all summer.
PRAIRIE-CLOVER, PURPLE Petalostemon purpurea	-	☼	16-20″ tall; fern-like deep green leaves; 1″-2″ tall rose to deep purple cones of blossoms in June till August.
PRIMROSE, EVENING Oenothera spp.	◌	☼	6-30″; yellow-white flowers.

Plant Name	Soil Moisture	Sun Tolerance	Description and Comments
PRIMROSE, MISSOURI Oenothera missouriensis	◯	☼	To 10-12″ tall; bright green leaves; large yellow flowers; flowers open in evening and last until late morning, often turning reddish-orange; mid-summer blooming.
PRINCE'S PLUME Stanleya pinnata	-	☼	2-5′ tall; blue-green leaves; plumes of yellow flowers from June to August.
SHASTA DAISY Chrysanthemum maximum	◑	✹ ☼	1′ in height; white blooms throughout the summer, starting in June.
SULPHUR FLOWER Eriogonum umbellatum	◯	☼	6-8″; sulfur-yellow flowers; evergreen leaves; forms a groundcover.
SUNROSE Helianthemum nummularium	◯	☼	Varieties of colors available; different foliage colors; height 8″.
RED HOT POKER Kniphofia uvaria	◯	☼	Spikes of small bright red flowers; 18″ in height and 15-18″ in spread.
TULIPS Tulipa spp.	◯	☼	A wide selection of this popular spring flower; requires less water than commonly believed.
YARROW, COMMON Achillea millefolium	◯	☼	8-16″ tall; fern like leaves; white to deep pink flowered cultivars available.
YARROW, TALL Achillea filipendulina	◯	☼	24-30″ tall; 24″ spread; many cultivars; seed heads used in dry arrangements; spreads.

Ground Covers and Vines
(low-growing 12″ or less; generally self-spreading)

Plant Name	Soil Moisture	Sun Tolerance	Description and Comments
BOWER, WESTERN VIRGINIA Clematis liguesticifolia	◯	✹ ☼	Deciduous rambling or climbing vine; numerous clusters of tiny white, fragrant flowers in summer; distinctive display of feathery fruits in fall; yellow fall color.
BUFFALO GOURD* Cucurbita foetidissema	-	✹ ☼	Hardy dryland vine.
CLOVER, ALSIKE Trifolium hybridum	◑	✹ ☼	Less than 3″; upright perennial; pink flowers.

Plant Name	Soil Moisture	Sun Tolerance	Description and Comments
DIANTHUS Dianthus caesius	◐	✹ ☼	Tight mounds; blue-green leaves; lavender-pink blooms; holds leaves in winter.
EUONYMUS, WINTERCREEPER Euonymus fortunei cv. 'Colorata'	◐	✹	Viney, deep green, broad-leaved evergreen; bronzy foliage in the winter.
FLEECE FLOWER, PINK Polygonum reneutria	◐	✹ ✹ ☼	Small pink flowers on stalk; 4" high; glossy turns bronze in winter.
FLEECE VINE, SILVERLACE Polygonum auberti	-	☼	Showy panicles of white flowers; very drought tolerant; reseeds readily.
GRAPE HOLLY, CREEPING OREGON Mahonia repens	○	✹ ✹ ☼	To 20"; broadleaf evergreen resembling holly; yellow bloom in the early spring; shades of bronze in the fall; edible blue-black fruit.
HENS 'N CHICKS Sempervivum	-	✹ ☼	Exceptionally drought-tolerant; good for rock walls and rock gardens; evergreen.
HONEYSUCKLE, HALL'S Lonicera japonica cv. 'Haliana'	○	✹ ✹ ☼	Vine; deep green foliage; white flowers.
ICEPLANT, HARDY (YELLOW) Delosperma nubigenum	○	☼	Fleshy, bright green evergreen leaves which turn a brilliant red during the winter; crystalline yellow flowers in the spring; quick growing.
ICEPLANT, HARDY (BLUE) Delosperma cooperi	○	☼	Same as delosperma nubigenum, but has bright blue-purple flowers; not as hardy as d. nubigenum.
IRIS, DWARF BEARDED Iris pumila	○	✹ ☼	Spring or summer bloom; 4-15"; some require shade.
JUNIPER, CREEPING Juniperus horizontalis (varieties)	●	☼	Many cultivated varieties available; slow to establish; evergreen.
JUNIPER, MOUNTAIN COMMON* Juniperus communis	○	✹ ✹	To 3' tall and 10' spread; needs partial shade; evergreen, bluish berries; varies in color and form; needs acidic soil.
KINNINNICK Aroctostaphylos uva-ursi	◐	✹ ✹	3"; broadleaf evergreen mat; pink and white flowers in late spring and early summer; red fruit; slow to establish.

Plant Name	Soil Moisture	Sun Tolerance	Description and Comments
LAMB'S EARS Stachys lanata	○	☼	8"; open foliage; aggressive spreader.
LAVENDER Lavandula vera	○	❋ ☼	6"; gray foliage; blue spike-like flowers.
GRAPE HOLLY, CREEPING OREGON Mahonia repens	○	❋ ❋ ☼	To 18"; broadleaf evergreen resembling holly; yellow blooms in early spring; shades of red in fall.
PENSTEMON, CREEPING RED Penstemon pinifolius	-	❋ ☼	4-6" flower stalks with red flowers; blooms all summer; needle-like semi-evergreen foliage.
PENSTEMON, ROCKY MOUNTAIN Penstemon strictus var. 'Bandera'	○	❋ ☼	10"-24" high; blue flowers.
PHLOX, CREEPING Phlox subulata	◐	☼	4" high and 24" spread; early spring, bright blue flowers.
PERWINKLE Vinca minor	◐	❋ ❋ ☼	Vine-like; broadleafed evergreen; deep green glossy leaves; blue flowers.
PLUMBAGO Ceratostigma plumbaginoides	◐	☼	Late summer purple flower; fall color; 8-12" high; 24" spread.
POTENTILLA, CREEPING Potentilla verna nana	○	❋	Tight mounds; buttercup flowers in summer.
PUSSYTOES Antennaria ssp.	-	☼	Less than 1" high; pink or white flowers; gray, evergreen foliage.
SEDUMS Sedum spp.	-	☼	3-8"; green or reddish fleshy leaves; red, yellow, pink and white flowers depending on species; evergreens; talk to local nursery about the wide variety of sedums available.
SNOW-IN-SUMMER Cerastium tomentosum	○	❋ ☼	6"; dense gray foliage; white flowers in early summer.
STRAWBERRY, DOMESTIC Fragaria varieties	◐	❋ ❋ ☼	Vine, white flowers with red berries.
STRAWBERRY, MOCK Duchesnea indica	○	❋ ❋ ☼	Yellow flowers and brillant nonedible red berries.
STRAWBERRY, WILD Fragaria americana	○	❋ ❋ ☼	2-4"; white flowers; edible fruit.

Plant Name	Soil Moisture	Sun Tolerance	Description and Comments
VERONICA, CREEPING Veronica repens	◯	☀	Small blue-purple flowers; 1″ high; aggressive spreader.
VIRGINIA CREEPER Parthenosiccus quinquefolia cv. 'Englemann'	◯	☀ ☆	Introduced; used as a vine but useful as ground cover on steep slopes; scarlet fall color; will climb walls.
VIRGINIA CREEPER Parthenosiccus inserta	◯	☀ ☆	Native; deciduous rambling vine; blue-black berries hang all winter; orange to scarlet fall color.
YARROW, DWARF* Achillea tomentosa cv. 'Nana'	-	☀ ☆	3-10″; flat heads of pink or yellow flowers from early spring to early fall; woolly leaves.

Maintenance

All landscaping, whether high water-requiring or drought-tolerant, requires maintenance. But with proper planning and design, maintenance costs and time can be reduced in low water-requiring landscapes in comparison to traditional landscapes. Here are some basic maintenance tips for any type of landscape:

— Remove weeds before they get large. Not only do they look bad, but they steal water from the desirable plants.

— Raise the height of the lawn mower. Mowing grass slightly taller will help the soil's temperature, help retain moisture and provide a natural mulch. Conventional turfgrasses such as Kentucky bluegrass, should be maintained at a two inch height. Keep the mower's blades sharp in order to avoid bruising the grass. Do not remove more than 1/3 of the leaf area, in order to avoid stressing the turf.

— Mulch around trees and shrubs to deter soil compaction and weed growth. Use of an organic mulch will also improve the soil. Mulches also control weeds that compete for water with desirable plants.

— Thin out crowded plants, since these groupings will require more irrigation. Look at the mass plantings from several different angles. Decide which plants can be removed in order to eliminate a "busy" effect and which plants should be kept in order to have a balanced mass grouping effect.

WATERING

In the Denver metro area, the average turf areas need up to 1" of precipitation and/or irrigation water per week in the spring and fall, and up to 1½" of precipitation and/or irrigation water per week in the summer.

For clay soils, the best watering schedule in the Denver metro area is to water every third day. For sandy soils, water every day during the early mornings. This then reduces the amount of water lost to evaporation or wind. Before watering, keep in mind the amount of rain that has fallen in the last several days and adjust the watering amount accordingly.

AERATION

For almost all established lawns, compaction or hardening of the soil is an eventual problem. The soil becomes hard after traffic has compacted and removed most of the soil's pore space. For areas with turf or groundcovers, the problem may become compounded with an excess of thatch. It is also difficult to improve soil in established lawns. Aeration allows homeowners to improve the soil, but it must be done regularly.

Aeration is the process of mechanically pulling out small plugs or cores of dirt, which allows the soil to have pockets of air. This then allows the soil to have more pore space for water, air and nutrients. To improve the soil, homeowners can "top-dress" the soil after it has been aerated.

Experts recommend that residential landscapes be aerated twice to three times a year. The best times to aerate a landscape are in the spring and fall. Avoid doing it in very hot days, in order to avoid stressing the turf.

Before aerating a lawn, the area must be thoroughly watered a day or two beforehand. Then with an aerator (which are available at most rental stores), vertically aerate the area. Then to be sure that all of the areas have been reached, run the aerator horizontally over the area.

There are several options for "top-dressing" a soil. Use a commercial fertilizer or some type of organic matter, like manure, compost or peat moss. Another option is to use the plugs themselves. If the plugs are broken into a mulch consistency, the mulch can be used as a suitable top-dressing without a lot of expense.

POWER-RAKING

Thatch is a layer of old leaf litter, stems and roots that have gradually built into a mulch at the soil level. Until thatch reaches ½" thick, it acts as mulch by lowering the soil's temperature and reducing moisture evaporation on the soil's surface. It also acts a "shock absorber" reducing the impact of traffic and compaction of the soil. But once the thatch reaches ½" thick or more, it can become a barrier to air and water getting down to the soil. If the thatch is more than ¾" of inch thick, power-raking might be the recommended course.

Sometimes the thatch from a turf or groundcover is more than ¾" thick. The grass then suffers, because air and water can't get down to the roots. The best short-term remedy is power-raking. This is taking a mechanical rake and pulling up the thatch. One warning because the thatch can be so thick, some grass roots may be actually growing within the thatch level. The turf area may look sparse and bruised after the power-raking is completed. For this same reason, **do not power-rake during the heat of the summer.**

It's a good idea to aerate on a regular basis, since aeration improves the soil. Power-raking should only be considered as a short-term solution when the thatch has grown to more than ¾" thick. Power-raking doesn't improve the soil, but rather reduces the thatch.

FERTILIZATION

Turf grass (and every type of plant material) needs nutrients in order to survive and thrive. Fertilization is a method where nutrients that a plant needs are incorporated within the soil. CSU recommends that a Kentucky Bluegrass lawn be fertilized four times a year with 1lb. of nitrogen per 1,000 sq. ft. of turf area per application. Alternative, low-water requiring grasses can get along with less nitrogen. The U.S. Soil Conservation Service recommends applying ¼lb. of nitrogen in the early summer and ¾lb. of nitrogen in the early fall for alternative grasses.

To figure out the amount of nitrogen in a fertilizer, look at the three numbers on the front of the bag, i.e. 20-10-5. The first number always refers to nitrogen. This number tells you what percentage of the total weight of the fertilizer bag is nitrogen. Nitrogen is the element most directly associated with green growth. But recent studies have shown that if nitrogen is applied to a cool-season grass such as Kentucky blue grass during the cool seasons of the year (fall and spring), stronger root growth develops. If nitrogen is applied to cool-season grasses in the summer, more leafy growth develops.

The second number on a fertilizer bag refers to the content of phosphorus (P_2O_5). Phosphate is associated with root growth. P_2O_5 signifies that only 44% is available in phosphorus. Phosphorus is needed to have a drought-tolerant turf with a strong, healthy root growth. But since phosphate stays immobile in the soil, the best way to apply phosphate is to rototill it in into the soil, as it is being prepared as a turf bed.

The last and final number refers to potassium or (K_2O). K_2O signifies that only 83% is available potassium. Potassium is needed for photosynthesis of the plant. This is the process where the plant creates energy for cell growth.

Since strong root growth is necessary for healthy, drought-tolerant turf, apply the fertilizer in the cool months of spring and the fall. Avoid applying fertilizer in the heat of the day. This reduces the chance for "burned" grass due to heat. It also eliminates fertilizer from drifting with the wind and away from the area.

Apply about half the fertilizer with straight lines across the turf area. Then to minimize missed spots and burning, apply the second half at right angles from the first rows.

Talk to a nurseryman about fertilizer needs of specific plant species. Check with local garden centers on different methods of applying the fertilizer, such as spreaders.

WINTER CARE FOR AN IRRIGATION SYSTEM

Before the first frost in the fall, it is important to drain the water out of the automatic irrigation system's pipes. If the water freezes within the system's pipes, the pipes may break and damage the entire system. To find the proper procedure for draining the irrigation system, consult the system's owner's manual or an irrigation specialist.

PROPER PRUNING

One of the more important components in a maintenance program is pruning trees and shrubs. The reasons for pruning include removal of dead and sick branches, elimination of crowded branches, allow for more passage of light and air, encourage more flowering and/or fruiting, and control of size. Pruning practices can vary depending on the type of tree and shrub.

Colorado State University Cooperative Extension offers service-in-action sheets on the proper methods of pruning deciduous trees, fruit trees, evergreens and shrubs. Contact the local county horticulture agent for a copy.

MORE MAINTENANCE INFORMATION AVAILABLE

For more maintenance tips and information, contact the local county Colorado State University Extension Service for information on fertilization, aeration and power-raking. The Aurora Utilities Department's Water Conservation Office also offers landscape maintenance workshops during the summer months.

Glossary

A

Acid soil: A soil with pH value less than 7.0. The term usually applies to the surface layer or to the root zone unless specified otherwise. The pH value may vary greatly depending on the method used.

Aeration: The process in which plugs of soil are removed in order to create more space for air. The rate of aeration depends on the volume and continuity of pore space in the soil.

Alkali: The term is applied to soluable salts, especially sulfates and chlorides of sodium, sodium and potassium, which are present in some soils in arid and semi-arid regions in sufficient quantities that could be detrimental to a lawn.

Alkaline soils: A soil has a pH value greater than 7.0. The terms is commonly applied to only the surface layer of the soil.

Annual plant: A plant that completes its life cycle and dies in one year or less.

Arboretum: A collection of plants, trees and shrubs grown for public enjoyment, education or research.

Arid: Regions or climates that lack sufficient moisture for crop production. The limits of precipitation vary according to temperature conditions, with an upper annual limit for cool regions as much as 15 to 20 inches.

Automatic Irrigation System: An irrigation system using timers or self-propulsion to reduce labor requirements in the application of irrigation water.

Available nutrient: That portion of any element or compound in the soil that readily can be absorbed and assimilated by growing plants.

Available water: The portion of water in a soil that can be absorbed by plant roots.

Available water capacity: The capacity of a soil to store available water for use by plants.

B

Berm: A dirt shelf or ledge that is typically at the top or bottom of a slope.

Biennial plant: A plant that requires up to 2 years to complete its life cycle and then dies.

Broadcast seeding: Scattering seed on the surface of the soil, in contrast to drill seeding in which seeds are placed in rows in the soil.

Bunchgrass: A grass that forms a bunch or tuft in its natural conditions.

C

Canopy: The cover of leaves and branches formed by the tops or crowns of plants, i.e. trees.

Channel: A stream or ditch that may carry water.

Clay: A pliable fine-grain soil. The soil particles are less than .002 millimeters in diameter.

Coarse texture: The soil texture exhibited by sands, loamy sands, and sandy loams, except very fine sandy loam.

Cobblestone: Rounded or sub-rounded coarse fragments of rock from 3 to 10 inches in diameter.

Compaction: Organic residues or a mixture of organic residues and soil that have been piled and allowed to undergo biological decomposition.

Conifer: A tree belong to the order Coniferae with cones and evergreen leaves shaped like needles or "scale-like".

Contour: An outline of a slope or mass.

Cool-season plant: A plant that makes its major growth during the cool portion of the year, primarily in the spring.

D

Deciduous plant: A plant that sheds all its leaves every year at a certain season.

Deep percolation: Water that percolates below the root zone and cannot be used by plants.

Drainage, soil: The horizontal movement of water through a soil.

Drill seeding: Plant seed with a drill in relatively narrow rows, generally less than a foot apart.

E

Effective precipitation: That portion of total precipitation that becomes available for plant growth. It does not include precipitation lost to deep percolation below the root zone or to surface runoff.

Erosion: The wearing away of the land's surface by running water, wind, ice or other geological agents.

Evaporation-transpiration rate: The amount of water that the plant has lost due to sun evaporation and plant transpiration (the water vapor that the plant releases). The E/T rate given in the local media is for the evaporation-transpiration rate of Kentucky bluegrass.

Evergreen: Perennial plants that are never entirely without green foliage.

Exposure: Direction with respect to points of a compass.

F

Fertility, soil: The quality of a soil that enables it to provide nutrients in adequate amounts and in proper balance for the growth of specified plants.

Fertilizer: Any organic or inorganic material of natural or synthetic origin that is added to the soil to supply elements necessary for the plant's growth.

Fertilizer, analysis: The percentage composition of fertilizer in terms of nitrogen, phosphorus and potassium. For example, a fertilizer with a 10-10-5 analysis (which would be shown on the front of the fertilizer bag) would contain 10% nitrogen (N), 10% phosphorus (as P_2O_5) and 5% potassium (K_2O). Other elements may also be included. With P_2O_5, only 44% of it is available phosporus. With potash, K_2o signifies that only 83% is available potassium.

Fine texture: Consisting of large quantities of fine particles of soil, particularly clay and silt. Includes sandy clay, silty clay and clay.

G

Germination: The initiation of growth of a young plant from seed.

Grade: The slope of a road, channel or natural ground.

Grass: A member of the botanical family gramineae, characterized by bladelike leaves arranged on the stem and jointed stems.

Greenbelt: A strip of land kept in its natural or relatively undeveloped state and which serves to break up continuous areas of urban development.

Groundwater: Water under the surface of the soil.

Growing season: The period of days between the last freeze in the spring and the first frost in the fall.

H

Herb: Any flowering plant except those developing persistent woody bases and stems above ground.

Humid: Weather that is characterized by a great deal of moisture in the atmosphere.

Humus: The usually dark-covered organic portion of the soil consisting of decomposed plant or animal matter.

I

Inorganic: Not composed of or involving living organisims or their remains or products, such as rocks or minerals. In scientific terms, materials that do not contain carbon compounds.

Introduced plant: A plant that is not native to the region.

Irrigation: The application of water to land for the purpose of growing plants.

L

Landscape: All natural features, such as slopes, perennials, groundcovers, trees and shrubs of the surroundings of a residence.

Land Use Plan: The key element of a city's or county's comprehensive plan that describes the recommended location and intensity of development for public and private land uses such as residential, commercial, industrial, recreational and agricultural.

Loam: Soil that chiefly contains sand, silt, clay and organic matter.

M

Manure: The excrement of animals in varying stages of decomposition.

Microclimate: The climatic condition of a small area resulting from the modification of the general climatic conditions of the area. This can be caused by such things as shade from trees and the reflection of the sun from nearby sidewalks.

N

Native: A species that is part of an area's original flora.

Naturalized plant: A plant introduced from other areas which has become established in and more or less adapted to a given region by long-continued growth in that region.

Nursery: A place where plants, such as trees, shrubs, vines and grasses, are propagated for transplanting or for use as stocks for grafting.

Nutrients: Elements essential as raw materials for plant growth and development, such as carbon, oxygen, nitrogen, etc.

O

Open space: A relatively undeveloped green area or wooded area within an urban setting.

Organic: Composed of or derived from living organisms. In scientific terms, composed of carbon compounds.

Organic matter: By-products from processing of animal or vegetable matters, such as compost, manure and peat moss.

Organic gardening: A system of gardening that utilizes organic wastes and composts to the exclusion of chemical fertilizers.

P

Peat: Unconsolidated soil material consisting largely of undecompsed or only slightly decomposed organic matter accumulated under conditions of excessive moisture.

Percolation: The downward movement of water through soil, especially the downward flow of water in saturated or nearly saturated soil.

Perennial plant: A plant that lives normally for 3 or more years.

Permeability, soil: The capacity of the soil to enable water or air to move through it.

Pesticide: Any chemical agent used for control of specific organisms, such as insecticides (for insects), herbicides (for weeds) and fungicides (for fungi).

pH: A numerical measure of acidity or alkalinity in soil or water. Neutral is pH 7.0. All pH values below 7.0 arc acid, and all above 7.0 are alkaline.

Plant nutrients: The elements or groups of elements taken in by a plant which are essential for its growth. These include nutrients obtained from fertilizers.

Precipitation: A general term for all forms of falling moisture, including rain, snow, hail and sleet.

Pure live seed: The product of the percentage of germination, plus the hard seed and the percentage of pure seed, divided by 100.

R

Reservoir: Impounded body of water or controlled lake in which water is collected or stored.

Retention pond: An area where precipitation is captured and held for later use in irrigation.

Root zone: The part of the soil that is penetrated or can be penetrated by plant roots.

S

Saline soil: Soil containing sufficient salts to impair its productivity.

Sand: Soil containing large particles between 0.05 to 2.0 millimeters in diameter.

Saturate: To fill all the voids between soil particles with liquid.

Saturation point: In soils, that point at which a soil will no longer absorb any amount of water without losing an equal amount.

Screening: The use of any vegetative planting, fencing, or other architectural treatment which will effetively hide from view any undesirable areas from the main traffic area.

Seedbed: The soil prepared by natural or artificial means to promote the germination of seed and growth of seedlings.

Semi-arid: A term applied to regions or climates where the natural moisture is normally greater than arid conditions but still definitely limits the growth of most plants.

Shrub: A wood perennial plant differing from a tree by its low stature and by generally producing more than one trunk.

Silt: Soil made of particles between .05 and .002 millimeter in diameter.

Slope: An upward or downward incline from the surface.

Sod-forming grass: Grasses that have stolons or rhizomes, and form a sod or dense mass.

Soil amendment: Any material, such as compost, peat moss or manures, that is worked into the soil to make it more amenable to plant growth.

Soil texture: The basic make-up or structure of a soil.
Sand: Soil material that contains 85% or more of sand.
Loam: Soil materials that contains a mixture of clay, silt and sand.
Clay: Soil materials that contains 40% or more of clay, less than 45% of sand, and less than 40% of silt.
Silt: Soil material contains 80% or more of silt and less than 12% of clay.

Stand: A grouping of trees or other plants occupying a specific area and sufficiently uniform in species, age and condition to be distinguishable from other plantings in the area.

Subgrade: The soil prepared and compacted to support a structure or a pavement system.

T

Terrace: An embankment or shelf that is constructed across a slope to control erosion by diverting or storing surface runoff instead of permitting it to flow uninterrupted down the slope.

Topsoil: The surface layer of a soil. It can also refer to the earthy material used as a top-dressing for residential lots.

Transpiration: The photosynthetic and physiological process by which plants release water into the air in the form of water vapor.

Tree: A woody perennial plant that reaches a mature height of at least 8 feet and has a well-defined stem. There is no clear-cut distinction between shrubs and trees. Some plants, such as Amur Maples, may grow as either trees or shrubs.

U

Urban Area: The U.S. Bureau of Census defines urban as towns of over 2,500.

V

Vegetation: Plants in general or the sum total of plant life in area.

W

Warm-season plant: A plant that completes most of its growth during the warm portion of the year, generally late spring and summer.

Water penetration: The depth to which irrigation water or rain penetrates soil before the rate of downward movement becomes negligible.

Weather: The state of the atmosphere at any given time with regard to precipitation, temperature, humidity, cloudiness, wind movement and barometric pressure.

Bibliography

Ashton, Ruth
 Plants of Zion National Park,
 Zion Natural History Association,
 Springdale, UT 1976
 Good photos

**Borland, James N., Sylvia Brockner &
Jeanne R. Janish**
 Native Plants of Genesee,
 Genesee Foundation, Golden, CO 1987
 Plants that work for the Foothills region

Coates, Margaret,
 Perennials for the Western Garden,
 Pruett Press, Boulder, CO 1976

Creasy, Rosalind,
 Complete Book of Edible Plants,
 Sierra Club, San Francisco, CA, 1982
 Covers almost all aspects of edible landscaping

Creasy, Rosalind,
 Cooking from the Garden,
 Sierra Club Books, San Francisco, CA 1988
 Recipes for produce from edible landscaping

Damrosch, Barbara
 Theme Gardens
 Workman Publishing, NY, NY 1982
 Illustrated ideas for theme gardens

Elmore, Francis H.,
 Shrubs and Trees of the Southwest Uplands,
 Southwestern Monuments Association, Tucson, AZ
 1976
 Current and historic uses of native plants in the SW

English, Sandal
 Fruits of the Desert,
 Arizona Daily Star, Tucson, AZ 1981
 Lots of useful recipes

**Harper, Pamela &
Frederick McGouerty,**
 Perennials,
 HP Books, Tucson, AZ 1985

Hillier, H.G.,
 Hillier's Colour Guide of Trees and Shrubs
 David and Charles Inc., North Pomfret, VT, 1981
 Reference for names and descriptions

Kelly, George,
 Rocky Mountain Horticulture,
 Pruett Press, Boulder, CO, 1967

Kelly, George,
 Wood Plants of Colorado
 Pruett Publishing, Boulder, CO 1970

Kourik, Robert, Ed. by Mark Kane,
 **Designing and Maintaining
 Your Edible Landscape Naturally,**
 Metamorphic Press, Santa Rosa, CA, 1986
 Tips on useful garden wisdom

Lamb, Samuel H.,
Woody Plants of the Southwest,
Sunstone Press, Santa Fe, NM, 1977

Niethammer, Carolyn
American Indian Food and Lore
Macmillan Publishing Co., NY, NY, 1974
Useful recipes for native CO plants

Phillips, Judith,
Southwestern Landscaping with Native Plants,
Museum of New Mexico Press, Santa Fe, NM, 1987
Information on native plant design

Reader's Digest Editors,
Practical Guide to Home Landscaping,
Readers' Digest Press, NY, NY, 197?
Covers all aspects of residential landscape design

Robinette, Gary O.,
**Water Conservation in
Landscape Design and Management,**
Van Nostrand Reinhold Co., 1984
Covers almost every topic on water conservation

Smith, Ken
**Home Landscaping
in the Northeast and Midwest,**
HP Books, Price Stern Publishing,
Los Angeles, CA, 1985
General text on residential landscape design

Smith, Shane,
Bountiful Solar Greenhouse,
John Muir Publications, Santa Rosa, CA 1982,
Thorough and addresses unheated conditions

Smyser, Carol
**Nature's Design:
A Practical Guide to Natural Landscaping,**
Rodale Publishing, Emmaus, PA 1982
Illustrated guide to natural landscaping

Stebbins, Robert L. and Lance Walheim,
Western Fruit, Berries and Nuts,
HP Books, Price Stern, Los Angeles, CA

Stuart, Malcolm,
Herbs and Herbalism,
Van Nostrand Reinhold, NY, NY 1980,
Text in various uses for common plants

Sunset Editors,
Sunset Western Garden Book,
Lane Publishng, Stanford, CA, 1979
Plants section is very useful

Tolley, Emelie and Chris Mead,
Herbs: Gardens, Decorations and Recipes,
Potter Books, Crown Publishing, NY, NY, 1985
How to use herbs in a planting design

University of California,
**Drip Irrigation
for the Home Garden and Landscape,**
University of California, Berkeley, CA, 1976

Weber, William,
Rocky Mountain Flora,
Colorado Associated University Press,
Boulder, CO, 1976
Widely used for taxonomic names

Williams, Kim,
Eating Wild Plants,
Mountain Press Publishing Co., Missoula, MT, 1976
Specific instructions on use of local plants

Addendum:

**Huddleston, S. and M. Hussey,
Grow Native:
Landscaping with Native and Apt Plants of the
Rocky Mountains**
Denver, CO, 1981

Aurora's Lawn Permit Ordinance

The average Aurora citizen uses 145 gallons of water each day. Half of this water (73 gallons) is used to water landscaping and lawns.

To help ensure more water-efficient landscaping and water for future Aurorans, a lawn permit ordinance was passed in Aurora in 1981. The ordinance requires that a specified amount of soil preparation must be added to the turf's soil and limits the amount of turf that may be installed as lawn.

The Aurora lawn ordinance requires, and experts recommend that soil preparation include a minimum of 3 cubic years of organic matter and 10lbs. of treble super phosphate per 1,000. The organic matter and the treble super phosphate need to be rototilled or disced into the soil to a minimum depth of six inches. Organic matter is defined by the ordinance as COMPOST, PEAT MOSS, AGED MANURES, AGED SAWDUST OR ANY COMBINATION OF THE ABOVE MATERIALS. Residents must bring in the receipts for the soil preparation materials before getting a permit.

The Lawn Permit Ordinance limits the amount of (Kentucky bluegrass) turf that a citizen may install in their lawn. When a resident applies for a lawn permit, he/she must bring a copy of his/her site plan or a map showing the dimensions of the total lot and the dimensions of where grass will be installed. The table for the turf limitation is:

Lot Size Square Feet	Maximum Sod Allowed Square Feet
4,000	2,600
4,500	2,750
5,000	2,900
5,500	3,050
6,000	3,200
6,500	3,350
7,000	3,500
7,500	3,575
8,000	3,650
8,500	3,725
9,000	3,800
9,500	3,875
10,000	3,950
10,500	4,025
11,000	4,100
11,500	4,175
12,000	4,250
12,500	4,325
13,000	4,400
13,500	4,475
14,000	4,550
14,500	4,625
15,000	4,700
15,500	4,775
16,000	4,850
16,500	4,925
17,000	5,000
Over 17,000	50% of the lot area not used for structures may be devoted to lawns.

For further information about the Lawn Permit Ordinance, contact the Aurora Utilities Department's Water Conservation Office.